Can I Come Home, Please?

IN ASSOCIATION WITH THE IMPERIAL WAR MUSEUM

Can I Come Home, Please?

The Second World War – by the
children who lived through it

Selected by Phil Robins

■ SCHOLASTIC

For two evacuees:
Pamela Robins, who lost her house but found a friend;
and Len Robins, who eventually ran away.

Scholastic Children's Books
Euston House, 24 Eversholt Street,
London, NW1 1DB, UK
A division of Scholastic UK Ltd
London ~ New York ~ Toronto ~ Sydney ~ Auckland
Mexico City ~ New Delhi ~ Hong Kong

First published in the UK as *Under Fire* by Scholastic Ltd, 2004
Published in the UK as *War Children* in 2005 by Scholastic Ltd
This edition published in the UK by Scholastic Ltd, 2009

All Sound Archive extracts © Imperial War Museum, 2004
Text copyright © Phil Robins, 2004

Cover image supplied by the Imperial War Museum

ISBN 978 1407 10903 9

All rights reserved
Printed and bound in the UK by CPI Mackays, Chatham, ME5 8TD

2 4 6 8 10 9 7 5 3 1

The right of Phil Robins to be identified as the author of this work has been asserted by him in accordance
with the Copyright, Designs and Patents Act, 1988.

Contents

Introduction   7

We lived in Hitler's Germany
(GERMANY: 1933–1938)   11

There's going to be a war
(GERMANY: 1938–1939)   37

What a strange holiday
(BRITAIN: 1–3 SEPTEMBER 1939)   63

No-man's-land
(BRITAIN: SEPTEMBER 1939–MAY 1940)   83

Closed in
(POLAND: 1939–1941)   101

Twenty-one miles
(BRITAIN: MAY–JUNE 1940)   123

On the seas and in the air
(BRITAIN: JULY–SEPTEMBER 1940)   141

When the bombing started
(BRITAIN: SEPTEMBER 1940–MAY 1941)   159

Taken away
(POLAND: 1941–1943)   183

If the trees could talk
(AUSCHWITZ: 1942–1944)   197

Losses on all fronts
(BRITAIN AND GERMANY: 1943–1945)   217

Ruins
(GERMANY: 1945)   243

Afterword   264

Suggested reading   266

Index of contributors   267

Index   269

Introduction

This book is about the Second World War (1939–1945), and consists mainly of the words of people who were children or teenagers at the time. The extracts that make up most of the text come from interviews recorded over the last 30 years by the Imperial War Museum and collected in its Sound Archive. The book tries to convey something of what children experienced during those years, and also to give a broad outline of the background events of the War itself.

The Second World War was just that – a world war that affected people in countries all around the globe. For reasons of space, and because of the nature of the Imperial War Museum's collections, this book deals mainly with northern Europe. However, although the War started in 1939, the first chapter actually begins in 1933 when Hitler came to power in Germany. This is because the events of the War only really make sense in the light of the six years of Nazi rule in Germany before it began. The story then moves between Britain, Poland – where the most terrible events took place – and Germany.

The War brought very different things to different people, depending on where they were and who they were, and this book tries to reflect that. For some children, the War was an adventure, while for others it was an unpleasant experience that had to be put up with. For many, it was an almost unimaginable ordeal. As a result, the stories in this book vary: some are light-hearted and some are sad; some are fairly trivial, others momentous; a number of them, inevitably, are upsetting.

Millions of children did not survive the War at all, but this book is made up of the words of those who did. In describing what they experienced, they also help to remember those who did not get the chance to tell their stories.

Notes

1 Some of the people featured in this book have changed their name in the years since they were children. Most of the Germans and Poles included here have moved to Britain since the War ended and a number of them have adopted British names. Many of the girls – British, German and Polish – have subsequently married and changed their names as a result. Where possible, I have given their original names, and a list at the back of the book gives their married or adopted names.

2 After several decades, people's memories are not always one hundred per cent accurate on every single detail, especially when they are talking about events that happened when they were small children. Nevertheless, the stories in this book have as far as possible been checked for historical accuracy and have been chosen because they represent common experiences.

Acknowledgements

For commissioning this book, and for all her subsequent suggestions and advice, I would like to thank my editor Lisa Edwards. Thanks also to Jill Sawyer for her dedication to the book; to Richard Smith for designing it; and to Kate Lockley for her picture research.

I am especially grateful to all those people whose wartime stories it has been a privilege to hear, and to the Imperial War Museum's Sound Archive for making them available. I would like to thank Margaret Brooks and her archive staff for their assistance, as well as Terry Charman, IWM historian, for his much-needed expertise.

Thanks, finally, to Leigh McAlea for all the ways in which she helped.

Germany 1918–1936

1918 The First World War ends, with Germany defeated. Britain, France and the United States blame Germany for the War and demand that it pay 'reparations' – large sums of money to make up for the damage. They redraw Germany's boundaries (taking away territory to reduce its power) and force it to get rid of most of its army. Many Germans feel angry and humiliated, including Austrian-born Adolf Hitler, who had served as a corporal in the German army during the War.

Early 1920s Germany is crippled by the demands imposed by the Allies. Unemployment hits record levels and the prices of food and other goods rise steeply, causing great hardship for ordinary Germans.

Mid 1920s Adolf Hitler, now the outspoken leader of the tiny National Socialist (or 'Nazi') Party, promises to make Germany strong again if he gets into power. In a book called Mein Kampf ('My Struggle') Hitler argues that the German people are a superior race who have a right to rule over others. He also blames the half a million Jews who live in Germany for many of its problems, including the loss of the First World War. His ideas are so extreme that few take him seriously.

1932 After a period of recovery in Germany, a worldwide economic crisis causes fresh problems and more than six million people are now unemployed. Various governments have come and gone, and now many people turn to Hitler's Nazi Party. In elections it gets more votes than any other.

1933 Hitler becomes the Chancellor of Germany (equivalent to the Prime Minister in Britain). He soon begins to rule by decree, without consulting the German Parliament. He bans all other political parties and has their leaders arrested. When the German President dies a year later, Hitler takes over his job as well. He also puts himself in personal charge of Germany's army. Hitler has now become a dictator, a ruler with absolute power.

1933–1935 As promised, Hitler brings jobs and economic stability to Germany. By restoring many Germans' pride in their country, Hitler becomes even more popular. Not everybody is taken in, but anyone who speaks out against him is severely punished.

1935 Nazi laws strip Jewish people of most of their rights, including the right to be treated as German citizens and the right to marry non-Jews. Since 1933, the Nazis have encouraged people to treat Jews with contempt. All over the country, signs have appeared in shops, restaurants and other public places saying 'No Jews'. Thousands of Jews have already left Germany, many moving to the United States.

1936 Hitler orders German troops into the part of Germany next to France known as the Rhineland. After the First World War, Germany had agreed to keep this area free from soldiers and it had later been occupied by British and French troops. Many Germans resented this, especially Hitler. But now Germany is beginning to flex its muscles again.

We lived in Hitler's Germany

Germany: 1933–1938

A tide of enthusiasm 12
A rousing song before lessons 16
Tiring on the arm 18
It was drummed into you 22
A gradual separation 25
People were very afraid 30
We're going to Shanghai 33

A tide of enthusiasm

When Adolf Hitler and his Nazi Party came to power in 1933, many Germans looked forward to a new era that would sweep away the hardship and difficulties that had dogged the country in the 1920s. Not everybody had voted for Hitler, and there were many who had their doubts about him, but he soon became extremely popular. Streets were festooned with bright red Nazi Party flags, thousands of people turned out at public rallies to cheer Hitler, and columns of uniformed Nazi Party members – known as 'Storm Troopers' – marched triumphantly through the streets. For most German children, it was an exciting time to grow up.

Wiebke Fick, from Kiel, aged 13 in 1933

It was all so lovely. You had these smartly dressed people and they were marching in nice lines through the town. And there was singing. And I loved that new flag, it was something very new. And it was a very bright scene in the towns when all the flags were flying. I was always pressing my parents to buy a flag. And we were just carried along [on] a tide of enthusiasm for this bright new thing that was coming along. We children, we were all like that, all my friends.

The Nazi flag was made up of a black swastika – an ancient cross-shaped symbol – on a white circle, with a deep red background. The Nazis hung enormous swastika banners from government buildings and in other prominent places. The flag became the German national flag in 1935.

Margarit Dierksen, from Hanover, aged 6 in 1933

My parents were never politically minded; we never heard anything of that at home. We were just a very happy family, [and we] just wanted

12

to be left to get on. But I do remember them telling me that when Hitler came to power things really improved in Germany; I always knew about that. [There were] lots of benefits and business was doing all right and Germany really, really got on its feet.

My parents had several holidays, and my dad went on a cruise to Norway and a cruise to Spain and, of course, after the inflation and all the money troubles, this was something really fantastic. Also I remember my father having a book and every month he paid a certain sum, and when the book was full he was entitled to exchange it for a *Volkswagen* 'Beetle'. Hitler thought everybody should be able to afford a car.

As a way of gaining popularity with working people, the Nazis came up with a scheme they called 'Strength Through Joy'. This offered cheap package holidays, which few Germans had ever experienced, as well as cheaper tickets for theatres and concerts. They also made plans to introduce one of the world's first cheap family cars – the *Volkswagen* (or 'People's Car') – though these plans were shelved when war broke out.

Girls belonging to the Hitler Youth movement on parade in Germany in the 1930s

Hitler wasn't satisfied with being popular. He wanted people to idolize him. So he encouraged everybody in Germany to call him their 'Führer' (which means 'Leader'), and introduced a new greeting that ensured his name was on people's lips every day.

Wiebke Fick
You greeted everybody with a Hitler salute. In the street, for instance, where in the past we would have done a little curtsey, and the little boys did a little bow and said *'Guten Morgen'* ['Good morning'] or whatever. Now it was *'Heil Hitler!'*

'*Heil Hitler*' means 'Hail Hitler' and is a bit like saying 'God save the Queen'. While saying it, Germans were also supposed to give the Nazi salute by raising their right arm at a 45°-angle with their palm outstreched.

Helena Pieper, from Dresden, aged 9 in 1933
When you went for rolls in the morning – this is a custom in Germany – you would go to the baker's and get fresh bread rolls which are really lovely and warm. And you shouldn't say, 'Good morning' [any more], you should say *'Heil Hitler'.*

Hitler's powerful voice and dazzling words about German greatness had an electrifying effect. Many people – especially teenagers – were thrilled by his talk of a glorious new era. And even younger children, though they didn't always understand or care about what he said, were easily caught up in the heated atmosphere.

Henry Metelmann, from Hamburg, aged 11 in 1933
Hitler, to me, was somebody like God. I really believed that man had enormous wisdom. He had a grasp of history. To me there was no greater human being.

Hitler being given flowers by a young girl

Margarit Dierksen

I remember he came to Hanover once in a big cavalcade, open Mercedes, and we all rushed to the main road to see him.

Even Jewish children, who would soon come to fear and loathe Hitler, were at first just as fascinated by him as anyone else.

Elisabeth Lukas, Jewish girl from Düsseldorf, aged 10 in 1933

Hitler came to Düsseldorf and every class contributed towards a flag. There was a big parade and I begged my father, '*Please* let me go with the class.' It hadn't sunk in at all.

15

So I went with the entire class and we stood for hours and hours on the street until finally he passed. I remember coming home and saying to my father, 'Hitler looked at me.' And he said, 'Yes, I'm sure. What a load of rubbish! Hitler looked at you!' Then the next day I found out that every one of these children was convinced that Hitler had looked at them.

A rousing song before lessons

For Hitler, children were the key to the future of Nazi Germany. He wanted to fill their minds with his ideas at an early age and bring up a generation of young Nazis ready and willing to follow his orders. So for Germany's children, there would be no getting away from the Führer – least of all in the classroom.

Anonymous girl, from Stuttgart, aged 2 in 1933
You had to sing Nazi songs and say *'Heil Hitler'* before lessons and after lessons. And [a picture of] Hitler hung over the teacher's desk, so you could look at him every day, all day long, if you wanted to.

Wiebke Fick
Every time we met a teacher [we] said *'Heil Hitler!'* – arm up. Every time a teacher came into the class we stood up. The teacher stood in front of the class, raised the arm and said, *'Heil Hitler!'* and we said, *'Heil Hitler!'* More often than not we also sang a rousing song before we started the lessons. I quite liked this. I'm very fond of singing.

■ ■ ■ ■ ■

Little girls giving the Nazi salute at a rally in Coburg, Germany, in 1934

Not all schoolteachers were supporters of the Nazi Party and many children could easily tell which ones were not fanatical about Hitler because they often just went through the motions of saluting and singing the Nazi anthems. But teachers who made trouble could lose their jobs and be replaced by others more enthusiastic about the new National Socialist lessons that were appearing on the timetable.

Wiebke Fick

We got a new headmistress. I didn't like her. None of us liked her. [And] we had no longer religious lessons. They disappeared from the timetable. We had instead what was laughingly called *Lebenskunde* which is something like 'Philosophy of Life'. But it didn't turn out to be like that. It was the most boring lesson, which was taken by the headmistress herself. And it was frightfully boring. What we learned, had to learn, or were supposed to learn, was all about the party. The history of the Nazi Party ... the life story of Hitler ... all the people in the Party – where they came from, what they'd done. It was terribly boring.

Henry Metelmann

History books were drawn in and new history books were issued. We were now told about German greatness. And also that Germany needed *Lebensraum* [living space] in the east because that was a Germanic right, to go to the east, because there is plenty of room. And after all we are the superior race – and the Slavic races, they are lower races. [And] we learned that Jews are a cancer in German society and most of the troubles we had, they could be led back to the Jews. [That was] my thinking in those days.

> Hitler had first spelled out these hateful ideas about race in his book, *Mein Kampf*, first published in 1925. He claimed that German-speaking people (which included Austrians) formed a separate, superior race. This Aryan 'master race' had become overcrowded in Germany and needed to expand by taking land (or 'living space') from neighbouring Poland and Russia (part of the Soviet Union), whose Slavic peoples were supposedly inferior.
>
> Hitler also claimed that Jews, who had lived in Europe for centuries, formed another separate race, even lower than the Slavs. He argued that those Jews living in Germany ruined the 'purity' of the Aryan race and made Germany weak.

■ ■ ■ ■ ■

Tiring on the arm

It wasn't just in the classroom that the Nazis tried to brainwash German children. They also used the Hitler Youth movement, a Nazi-run scout group that had sections for both boys and girls. As well as training them for military service, the Hitler Youth provided children with opportunities to take part in all sorts of new activities, and though it didn't appeal to everybody, it was very popular.

Henry Metelmann

Nowadays one says, 'Oh, we lived in Hitler's Germany – it must have been terrible.' But it wasn't, not for me, as a boy. Being in the Hitler Youth, we sometimes went to camps, once or twice a year – to the seaside or to the mountains. Of course we had to learn to march and learn military commands but there was plenty of fun too. We now played football or went swimming and things like that. In the street we boys had been so poor we seldom had a football to play with, and now in the Hitler Youth we had all these things. That was great.

A Hitler Youth parade

Margarit Dierksen

[It was] fantastic. We had bags and bags of sport. We went swimming, we went camping – it really was wonderful. Leaving the political side out of it, for me it was lovely. And being an only child, I had loads of friends. I was only in there for the sport, which I really enjoyed.

Sport was important to Hitler, who wanted to prove that Aryans were fitter and stronger than everybody else. In 1936 Germany hosted the Olympic Games in Berlin, and the Nazis used the event to glorify Germany and its youth. Germany did win more gold medals than any other country, but when the 'racially inferior' African-American Jesse Owens won four gold medals for athletics Hitler was furious.

Waltraudt Asser

A lot of it was sporty and physical and I wasn't like that. I found it such a drag. If somebody could jump that high or do something fantastic in sports it just didn't impress me. But you gradually got the idea that if you were ugly-looking or you weren't quite tall enough, then you weren't going to make it with the Nazis anyway.

■ ■ ■ ■ ■

Hitler Youth membership did not become compulsory until the War began in 1939, but all 'Aryan' children were strongly encouraged to join the ranks. Once they had enrolled, marching and standing to attention became a way of life, and though some found this dull, many enjoyed the sense of belonging.

Margarit Dierksen

If there was a parade, you had to be on duty, you had to enter in – you couldn't just say, 'Well no, I'm not coming.' It was just something you belonged to and you did everything with them.

Wiebke Fick

It was very tiring on the arm, because you sang the national anthem and then you sang the 'Horst Wessel [Song]', and then the Hitler Youth anthem. And all the while through all the verses you had to stand like that with your arm outstretched and up.

The 'Horst Wessel Song' – named after a Berlin Storm Trooper leader – was a marching song that glorified Germany and its *Führer*.

Wiebke Fick

We were called upon to carry water at [Nazi rallies] which was quite fun. We used to cart these huge buckets of water around with a metal mug clipped to the side. And we used to go round reviving those who had fainted in the hysteria, which we thought was quite fun. The ministering angels in these mass meetings. It was very infectious – *'Sieg Heil!'* and shouting. And the whole atmosphere was terrific.

The main Nazi Party rally took place every year in Nuremberg. It was designed to impress people with the sheer scale of the Nazi movement and hundreds of thousands of people took part, including many Hitler Youth members. *'Sieg Heil!'* means 'To Victory!' and at Nazi rallies it was chanted over and over again by excited crowds while they gave the Hitler salute.

Hitler Youth boys with flags at a Nazi rally

Wiebke Fick

The whole movement of course was unifying because there were no outsiders to our view. Everybody was in it. And everybody was there. And everybody wore the uniform. And everybody sang. That was certainly very unifying, yes.

It was drummed into you

In fact there were plenty of 'outsiders' in Hitler's Germany, where those who were not 'Aryan' were excluded from many aspects of life, including the Hitler Youth.

Jews had lived in Germany for generations and though they had a different religion from the Christian majority, they considered themselves to be just as German as anyone else. But Hitler wanted people to think of Jews as dangerous outsiders who were a threat to German society and to the 'purity' of the Aryan race. He tried to persuade people that Jews – many of whom were successful in business and relatively well off – had stolen their money from Aryans and were secretly plotting to ruin the country.

Under the Nazis, hatred of Jews (which is usually known as 'anti-Semitism') was encouraged in all sorts of ways, not just at school. Much of this was the work of Josef Goebbels, Hitler's Minister of Propaganda. (Propaganda is the deliberate and organized spreading of a particular political idea.) He tightly controlled all German newspapers, radio broadcasts and cinema newsreels, and used them over and over again to drive home Hitler's ideas about politics and race.

Hildegard Hornblower, from Hanover, aged 13 in 1933

You soon became aware of the propaganda of the 'master race'. In fact it was drummed into you so much that you'd have to be blind and deaf not to be aware of it. Suddenly all inventions that had been made from the wheel onwards, they were made by Germans! A lot of people simply believed the propaganda. They believed that all Jewish people were terribly rich and out to steal your hard-earned pennies away. Or else sully the pure German blood.

The Nazis had started a special newspaper – Der Stürmer – devoted entirely to the subject of Jews. They pinned it up on street corners and in railway stations all over Germany. It was supposed to encourage people to think of Jews as ugly and dangerous and it always contained insulting drawings of them.

A front page from Der Stürmer newspaper

Gisela Spanglet, from Berlin, aged 8 in 1933

One saw this display of the newspaper, *Der Stürmer*, full of these anti-Semitic things. They were always done in display cabinets. You had no excuse for not seeing them because you could not afford to read the paper, because it was all there for you. We used to stand there and read all these things and look at the pictures. And that was really quite extraordinary too because we didn't know anyone who looked like that, or had a nose like that, or lips like that. And I remember reading that Jews also smell of onion and garlic. I mean, we didn't know people like that!

The Nazis also used the Hitler Youth movement to spread their propaganda and young children were brainwashed into repeating anti-Semitic slogans and taking part in demonstrations against Jews.

People are prevented from buying from a Jewish shop

Wiebke Fick

We were actually as little girls marching through the streets with our flags singing, '*Ja, wann das Juden blüt…*' which means: 'Yes, when the Jewish blood splashes from the knives things will go twice as well.' Not always, of course. There were other nice hiking songs. But this was one [song]. It's horrifying.

Henry Metelmann

I must have been somewhere around 12, 13, with the Hitler Youth. Together with the [Storm Troopers], we went to Jewish shops in town – one was called Finkel's, a large department store. And we stood outside and kind of prevented shoppers going in to buy. And I stood there, and it was all great big fun to me to stand with the [Storm Troopers] together, and I felt important. What it really meant, I didn't have much idea.

In 1933, the Nazis organized a nationwide boycott of Jewish-owned shops and businesses, and similar local boycotts were organized in later years. Nazi Storm Troopers, sometimes aided by Hitler Youth boys, stood menacingly outside and told would-be customers to spend their money in 'Aryan' shops instead. They hoped to put Jews out of business and force them to leave the country.

A gradual separation

Gradually the propaganda began to have an effect, and as harsh new Nazi laws stripped away Jews' rights – including the right to be treated as German citizens and the right to marry Aryans – more and more ordinary Germans also began to turn against them. All over the country, signs saying 'No Jews' and 'Jews not welcome' went up in the windows of shops, restaurants and hotels. Jews were increasingly jeered at in the street and sometimes beaten up.

Not everybody was anti-Semitic, but with Nazi Storm Troopers patrolling the streets, even people who weren't taken in by the propaganda found it more and more difficult to be openly friendly to their Jewish neighbours. This was something that children did not always understand.

Anonymous girl, Stuttgart

When we lived in the suburb we had quite a few Jews lived there. And there was one chap, with a long white beard, and he had a lovely garden with roses in it. And his name had something to do with roses – Rosenberg or Rosenthal or something like that – and I remember I would go by and say hello to him. Well, one day I went by and said hello to him [and] he just looked away. And I went home and I was very upset and I said to my mother, 'He doesn't talk to me. What have I done wrong? What's the matter?'

The banner across this street says, 'Jews are not wanted here'

For Jewish children themselves, life in Hitler's Germany became extremely difficult, especially at school.

Susan Oppenheimer, Jewish girl from Nuremberg, aged 10 in 1933

We had always met, two or three of us, to go to school together and [we] said, 'Good morning.' And suddenly it started that [my friend] put out her right arm, *'Heil Hitler!'* And the others would say, *'Heil Hitler!'* And I would still say, 'Good morning'. But eventually I didn't go with them any more because I thought it's only going to cause problems to me. [And] gradually there was a sort of separation. There were some children who used to call, 'Stinking Jew!' And I used to say, 'Well, I am a Jew but *you* stink!' And that caused some fights.

Although there were a few Jewish-run schools in Germany, most Jewish children went to ordinary state schools where they mixed with other German children. About one per cent of German schoolchildren were Jewish, so they were very much in the minority.

Elisabeth Lukas

There were two other Jewish girls in my class. And we got together and decided beforehand [that when the teacher came in] we would stand up like always, but we would certainly not lift our right arm.

And for the first few days we had a number of teachers, no one objected. Everybody was very civilized about it, until on the third or fourth day we had a lesson [and] the teacher was obviously a Nazi. And she came in, did the Nazi salute. She surveyed the class. There were all these little tots stood with their arms raised. And then she said in a loud voice which I hear to this day, *'Ich sehe noch nicht alle Hände,'* which means 'I do not yet see all hands.'

Whereupon she put her arm down, so did the children. No one sat down. She then raised her arm again. The others raised their arm again. The three little Jewish girls didn't. It was a complete repeat performance. After the second time we three – who were not sitting near to one another – sort of looked at one another. There was nothing we could do about it.

So the third time we raised our hand, whereupon she agreed for the class to sit down. And from then onwards for the rest of my schooldays with this particular teacher we three Jewish girls made the Hitler salute.

Barbara Isralowitz, Jewish girl from Bielefeld, aged 10 in 1933

I was chosen to represent the county in running for my age group. And the night before we were to go to this place my parents had a letter to say would they please withdraw me because it would be 'inappropriate'. They didn't want a person with a Jewish name.

Susan Oppenheimer

I used to write good essays, and before Hitler I used to sometimes get a form prize or something like that. And I suddenly got very bad marks. The teacher we had was a member of the Storm Troopers and he simply said, 'Jews can't write good German. Therefore you cannot have a good essay.'

I think, on the whole, I didn't let it get me down. And there was always great support at home. My father would talk about Jewish Nobel Prize winners and Jewish musicians and artists and point out the high proportion of Jews in that field. He instilled a pride in us being Jewish and [in] Jewish history. My parents weren't religious Jews but they were entirely conscious Jews.

Certainly my father was proud of being Jewish. I'm not sure about my mother, I think maybe she thought it was a bit inconvenient.

■ ■ ■ ■ ■

Most German Jews were proud of their Jewish history and culture, but not all of them had the same beliefs. Some families practised their religion in a very traditional way, and brought up their children strictly according to Jewish custom. Others were more informal, and some were not religious at all. (A few had even been baptized as Christians, preferring to blend in completely with other Germans.) None of this made any difference to Hitler, who wasn't interested in religion. He thought of Jews only in terms of their 'race', and hated all of them equally.

An anti-Semitic cartoon from a children's school book

Ruth Heilbron, Jewish girl from Lingen, aged 10 in 1933

We had teachers at this school who were very pro-Nazi and I was the only Jewish girl. And this particular teacher made my life a misery. She told all the girls not to talk to me. During the intervals I stood on my own in the playground. Some of the teachers came to talk to me out of pity but were afraid of this one teacher because she might denounce them. She arranged that I would sit right at the back of the class and two rows were left vacant and I sat against the wall.

[And] this teacher, who was headmistress, she brought in big cardboard pictures of Jews, with big noses, flat feet, big bellies, bushy eyebrows. And she said, 'These are the Jews, these are the vermin of society, they have to be destroyed.' And one girl got up and said, 'But Ruth Heilbron doesn't look like that. Neither do her parents. Nor the other Jewish people in this town.' So she got lines to write and was sent out of the class.

As part of the racial 'lessons' given by the Nazis, schoolchildren were told that pure Aryan children had beautiful blond hair and blue eyes but Jewish children were ugly. Pictures like those in *Der Stürmer* were sometimes used to make the point.

People were very afraid

Jews were not the only people to suffer in Nazi Germany. Gypsies, Jehovah's Witnesses and gay people were among other minority groups that Hitler persecuted. Increasingly he used his secret police – known as the Gestapo – to arrest them or terrorize them in their homes.

Magdalena Kusserow, Jehovah's Witness from Bad Lippspringe, aged 10 in 1933

Fifteen, sixteen, eighteen times the Gestapo came to look in our house for literature. My brother, he'd look through the window and then he'd say, 'The Gestapo comes! The Gestapo comes!' Then we hid the Bible, even the Bible. We put it under the cupboard. My mother said, 'They are too lazy, they don't like to bow down.' So we hid some literature under the boards on the floor.

Jehovah's Witnesses are a Christian group whose beliefs differ from those of most mainstream Christians. The Nazi Party, who claimed to represent true German Christians, banned the Jehovah's Witnesses by law. Many of them were arrested.

Together with more and more Jews, the Nazis sent many of these people to prisons and to newly built 'concentration camps' (so-called because large numbers of people were concentrated there). These consisted of barracks surrounded by barbed-wire fences. Conditions inside were appalling and many prisoners died, but the Nazis told people that they were merely work camps for the lazy.

Henry Metelmann

I was in favour of the whole Nazi thing and I was very much in favour of the *Führer* and the greatness of Germany. That all appealed to me. My attitude was, 'Well, all these second-rate people like Jews and gypsies and layabouts and Bible punchers and homosexuals, and all these lower elements who don't want to work, yes, get them into a concentration camp and make them work! That's good for Germany, and serves them right!'

That was my attitude and I saw nothing wrong with it. I thought, 'Yes, a good thing, concentration camps.'

Anonymous girl, Stuttgart

Once I saw a man being taken to the police station. I was going to kindergarten with my sister, we passed the police station, and next to it there's a woman officer who gave us sweeties, and we would always stop there and look at her and say hello. And a police van came up and they grabbed a man out and they kicked him into the station. And I was horror-struck by it and the woman said, 'That's a Jew. He's going to prison.'

The Nazis also arrested their political opponents, including many members of the left-wing Communist Party. (In Russia, Communists had taken over after a revolution in 1917 and in Germany during the 1920s Communists and Nazis had openly fought in the streets as they struggled for political control of the country. As soon as he came to power Hitler began to arrest and murder Communists whom he hated almost as much as Jews.)

Henry Metelmann

We had a neighbour, his name was Eycken. And Herr [Mr] Eycken was something like a secretary of the union, down by the docks. Whether he was a Communist, I do not know, but he must have been a left-wing man. And one morning Herr Eycken had been taken away in the night. They came early in the morning, police and [Storm Troopers], and he was taken away. And later on it materialized he was in a concentration camp.

Well, I liked Herr Eycken. I did not want to say anything against Herr Eycken because he always had been good to me. So there was a slight contradiction in my mind about that – 'Why did they take Eycken away?' But then I thought, 'Well, the big ones, they must know what's good for Germany.'

And my father, whenever he said something which was against the regime, which he sometimes did, it just came out, he said, 'Now, Henry, don't go out in the street and say what I have said because then the same will happen to me as happened to Herr Eycken and you would not like that, would you?'

People were expected to place their loyalty to the Führer above other considerations, and the Gestapo encouraged people to inform on friends and neighbours who said things against Hitler. Through the Hitler Youth, they even encouraged children to denounce their parents if they expressed anti-Nazi views. Despite all this, there were a few people who did dare to speak out.

Heinz Spanglet, Jewish boy from Berlin, arrested by the Gestapo in 1934, aged 16

A group of friends formed a little group and we printed leaflets with very primitive means. We stuck little notices on lampposts, proclaiming anti-Nazi views. I was picked up by the Gestapo together with some other friends and we disappeared from the scene for two weeks and our parents didn't know where we were. We were taken first to the Gestapo headquarters in Berlin. Of course we were beaten up when we arrived, in the routine manner. From there [we were taken] to a prison for 'political offenders' of all kinds. Anybody who was an anti-Nazi was liable to land up there. I was there for at least a week in solitary confinement, which at the age of 16 was quite an experience.

We're going to Shanghai

Among Jews in Germany, opinion was divided about emigration. Was it better to stay put and hope the Nazi era would pass? Or to leave home and try to make a new life in an unknown country? Many Jews had decided to leave soon after Hitler came to power. Others felt it was better to bide their time, thinking that things surely couldn't get any worse.

Gerda Ballin, from Munich, aged 17 in 1933 when she came to Britain

My father's opinion was that he must leave as soon as possible because he had a very good foretaste of what was to come. And he was laughed at a lot, made fun of by other Jewish people and friends and so on. They said, 'Why are you so pessimistic?'

Between 1933 and 1938 about 130,000 Jewish people – roughly a quarter of the total Jewish population of Germany – left the country.

Waltraudt Asser, non-Jewish girl from Berlin, aged 8 in 1935

We had many Jewish friends [at school]. And it was pretty early on when they came to say goodbye, those that could afford to go. They said, 'We're going to Shanghai,' 'We're going to America', 'We're going to…' wherever they managed to go. Well, you knew it wasn't because they *wanted* to go.

Shanghai, in China, was one popular destination for Jews fleeing Germany, as it was one of the only places where a visa for entry was not required. Nevertheless more Jews went to the United States than to any other country.

Elisabeth Lukas, emigrated with her family to Belgium in 1933

[My father] came first, to prepare things. And my mother, my brother and I followed. I had a frog in a jam jar with a little wooden ladder in it. And the day before we emigrated I spent the entire afternoon [catching] flies for this frog, which must be the only frog to have emigrated and left Germany because of Hitler.

■ ■ ■ ■ ■

Germany 1938–1939

March 1938 Hitler sends his troops across the border into Austria and takes over the Government. Many Austrians rejoice as their country becomes part of a new 'Greater Germany' but Austria's Jews now become subject to Nazi persecution.

The Nazis make life increasingly difficult for Jews in Germany and more of them try to leave. This suits Hitler, who wants a Germany that is entirely 'Judenrein' – 'free of Jews'. However, many countries, including Britain and the United States, will only let in a limited number of refugees.

July 1938 At a conference in France, representatives of 32 nations express sympathy for the Jews suffering under the Nazis – but none offers to make a significant increase in the number of refugees they will let in.

September 1938 Hitler is threatening to invade Czechoslovakia. Desperate to avoid war, British Prime Minister Neville Chamberlain flies to Munich and joins the leaders of France and Italy for emergency talks with Hitler. They reach an agreement that allows Germany to take over a small part of Czechoslovakia (close to the German border), but not all of it. Chamberlain returns to Britain announcing peace, but many Czechs feel betrayed by Britain and France for allowing Hitler to get his way.

9–10 November 1938 The Nazis organize a nationwide attack on Jewish property. Shops, businesses, private homes and synagogues are smashed up and looted, and several thousand Jewish men are arrested. The event later becomes known as 'Kristallnacht' – 'The Night of Broken Glass'.

November–December 1938 All Jewish children are expelled from state schools throughout Greater Germany. Jews are also banned from cinemas, theatres, art galleries and concert halls. Many Jewish businesses are confiscated. Most Jews are now desperate to escape from Nazi Germany, but many are unable to get a visa to enter another country.

November 1938 Britain agrees to a special rescue plan for refugee children. Over the following year, around 10,000 children escape to Britain on what become known as the 'Kindertransports' ('child transports'), but their parents have to remain in Nazi Germany.

March 1939 Hitler breaks the Munich Agreement, and sends troops further into Czechoslovakia. Much of the country, including the Czech capital, Prague, is absorbed into Greater Germany. Britain and France do nothing but protest.

Summer 1939 Hitler turns his attention to Poland, another country neighbouring Germany. He makes it clear he wants to occupy Poland and give its 'living space' to Germans. Britain and France promise that this time they will not stand by and do nothing if Hitler invades. All over Europe, people prepare themselves for war.

There's going to be a war

Germany: 1938–1939

Things are happening 38

Broken, smashed and destroyed 42

I wanted to get out 45

He's going to look at my sandwich 49

How nicely English people live! 54

What a great power 59

Things are happening

Hitler controlled Germany with an iron grip. Now he wanted to create a bigger, stronger Germany that would dominate Europe and the world beyond. In particular, he had always longed to unite Germany with its German-speaking neighbour Austria, where he had been born. So in March 1938 he sent in columns of troops, took over the Government and declared that the two nations were now united as a single 'Greater Germany'. It was a proud moment for many Germans.

German troops enter Austria in March 1938

■ ■ ■ ■ ■

Henry Metelmann, from Hamburg, aged 15 in 1938

They showed us at school that because Hitler was an Austrian he had taken Austria into our country, and somehow when I looked at the map and Germany was becoming bigger, I liked the idea!

The union was also welcomed in Austria, where the Nazis were popular – and where many people hoped for a share in the glorious future that Hitler spoke about so often. For those who opposed the Nazis, however, the takeover was a catastrophe.

Dorothy Oppenheimer, Jewish girl from Vienna, aged 10 when Hitler took over

Of course, things changed dramatically at school. I remember the teacher telling the children that we have a new regime now and you'll have noticed that things are different and I want you to promise me that you will come and tell me if you hear your parents saying anything nasty about this new regime that we have – you're to come and report to me.

Austrian Jews found themselves treated even more harshly than the Jews in Germany itself. Many were sacked from their jobs. Others had their homes broken into and looted. Some were forced by the Nazis to do humiliating work such as scrubbing the streets while crowds gathered round to watch.

Herbert Eisenthal, Jewish boy from Vienna, aged 13 when Hitler took over

Within days of Hitler walking in, you would find the janitor in the building where you lived would give you a mop bucket and say, 'Clean the stairs!' It was not physically difficult, but it was humiliating. I was amazed that you couldn't do anything about it, but I was told that if you did that and he called in a policeman you could be sent to a concentration camp or they would beat you up and there would be no questions asked.

Jewish men being forced to scrub the streets of Vienna
while a laughing crowd watches them

Once he'd grabbed Austria, Hitler soon turned his attention to Czechoslovakia, another of Germany's neighbours, and one that was now surrounded on three sides by German territory. Many German-speakers lived in Czechoslovakia, near the German border, and Hitler thought these areas should belong to Germany.

Henry Metelmann

Czechoslovakia was sticking out like a sore thumb, into the middle of Germany. And the propaganda line also started in the papers, showing that from Czechoslovakia, Germany could be attacked by air. Then there was propaganda that the Czechs had suddenly started treating the Germans badly.

Britain and France were against Hitler's plans for Czechoslovakia but they were desperate to avoid a costly war with Germany. So in September 1938 Neville Chamberlain and Edouard Daladier, Prime Ministers of Britain and France, went to Munich for emergency talks with Hitler.

Maria Siegel, Jewish girl from Munich, aged 13

I saw crowds and crowds of people moving in one direction and I just asked people, 'What's happening?' And they said something about a meeting and I rushed back to my grandmother's flat, because I was very short, and I said, 'Can I borrow your kitchen stool?'

And off I went to where everybody else went and there was an army lorry and that's about as near as I could get. I stood on my stool and one of the soldiers hauled me up on this army lorry, so I could see better. I saw all these guys arrive and people said, 'This is Daladier and this is Chamberlain – he's English you know.'

So presently I said thank you to the soldier, got down [off] my stool and went home. I thought, 'This is exciting, things are happening.'

In Munich, Chamberlain and Daladier reluctantly agreed that Hitler could have the border areas of Czechoslovakia, as long as he promised to go no further. In Britain, some people felt that the Czechs had been badly let down, while others celebrated the fact that war had been avoided. Chamberlain himself arrived back in Britain proclaiming 'peace for our time', but not everybody was convinced.

Maria Siegel

There was a lot of digging going on in the street outside and people said, 'They're preparing a subway' – an underground train, because Munich didn't have one. And then we heard murmurs from other sources: 'That's not going to be an underground. That's going to be a shelter. There's going to be a war.'

Broken, smashed and destroyed

On 7 November 1938, a teenaged Jewish refugee named Herschel Grynszpan shot a German official in Paris. Hitler had recently thrown the boy's parents out of Germany, along with thousands of other immigrant Polish families, and this was his response. The official died two days later and the Nazis used the episode to launch a violent attack on Jews throughout Greater Germany.

On 9 November gangs of Nazi Storm Troopers burned and looted Jewish properties and terrorized their owners. The Nazis claimed the violence was a spontaneous reaction by German citizens who were angry with Jews, but in fact they had carefully planned and organized it themselves. Although Jews had grown familiar with Nazi hatred, few were prepared for anything quite like this.

Margie Oppenheimer, from Westphalia, aged 14

I went to bed and about 11 o'clock I heard the singing and didn't pay much attention to it. All of a sudden there is a Nazi standing in front of me with a rifle in my face saying, 'Get up and get dressed.' 'I'm not dressing myself in front of you,' [I said.] I don't know where I got the guts to say that. He said, 'Get up and get dressed' and he went to my brother and told him the same thing. He went out of the room, but then you could hear the glass being smashed downstairs, all the windows being smashed.

Susan Oppenheimer, Jewish girl, from Nuremberg, aged 15

During the night men came bursting into our house and started smashing up everything. And everything that we had was broken, smashed and destroyed.

Anti-Semitic graffiti scrawled on a Jewish shop in Vienna

Walter Rechnitzer, Jewish boy from Vienna, aged 11

I suddenly saw all these books being burned in the street and I saw the synagogue on fire. I thought, 'My goodness, what's going on here?' Then I heard this man calling out and I saw a couple of men in uniforms beating up this chap. I ran forward and I saw it was my uncle. I wasn't a brave person – I used to run away from fights – but I went forward to try and help him. Unfortunately I got beaten up as well.

Because of all the smashed windows, 9 November 1938 later became known as 'Kristallnacht' ('The Night of Broken Glass'). During that single night, 91 Jews were murdered, hundreds of synagogues were burned down, thousands of shops and businesses were destroyed and some 30,000 Jews (mostly men) were arrested and taken to concentration camps. Storm Troopers had committed most of the violence but a few ordinary Germans had also been persuaded to take part. Most Germans were horrified and ashamed by what had happened, but they were too frightened of the Nazis to protest.

A Berlin synagogue in ruins after Kristallnacht, November 1938

Waltraudt Asser, non-Jewish girl from Berlin, aged 11

I saw their property ruined and the looting [that] went on afterwards. Shops were smashed. It was oil paint they used to put on the pavement in front of the shops. It was always something obscene like 'Jewish pig'.

Margarit Dierksen, non-Jewish girl from Hanover, aged 11
In the morning on the way to school, we saw the synagogue was burned down – it was still burning, all the shops were smashed. Everybody was talking about it, but you had to be a bit careful what you said. You couldn't take sides, you just kept very quiet about it. From then on, the Jews started disappearing. There weren't many Jewish shops left and these people came in for a lot of nastiness.

I wanted to get out

Getting out of Germany now became the priority for almost all remaining Jews. But emigration was expensive and difficult to organize. Despite international outrage at Nazi behaviour towards Jews – especially after Kristallnacht, *which was widely reported – many countries, including Britain and the United States, would only admit a limited number of refugees because they feared that they would be 'flooded'. Escape grew more difficult just as the need for it became more urgent.*

Barbara Isralowitz, Jewish girl from Bielefeld, aged 14 in 1937 when she wrote to Chamberlain
My father was afraid of being arrested and he just didn't feel safe. Life was totally impossible for him in Germany. And I was very much aware of that. And I had the idea to write to the British Prime Minister to tell him how wrong all this was and that my father should be allowed to come to England. And so I composed [a letter] in my school English and I wrote to Neville Chamberlain. And I just posted it in the ordinary way. And one day to my absolute amazement my parents said, 'There's a letter for you.' And I opened it and unfortunately it was very non-committal. It didn't really say anything, it merely referred me to the proper channels.

By November 1938, the Nazis were introducing new anti-Jewish laws almost every week. They forced Jews to have their passports stamped with a large 'J', restricted the times when they could travel and forbade them to have driving licences. They expelled all Jewish children from German state schools and forbade Jews from going to cinemas, theatres and other public places. They also began to confiscate more and more Jewish property, or else forced Jews to sell it to them at low rates. This meant that Jews who did leave could take nothing with them. In many cases even their bank accounts were seized.

Dorothy Oppenheimer

Some men with leather coats came into my father's shop and said, 'Mr Oppenheimer, you have to go home now. We'll take over the business now.' They took it over as a going concern in a prime position and that was that. They took both the shops. He no longer had a means of livelihood.

Maria Siegel

I was no longer able to go to school. [The] Jewish school was burnt down and Jewish children were forbidden to be taught. In addition to that we were turfed out of our flat, but I thought anything new was interesting and I didn't feel particularly deprived.

My father, being a lawyer and no longer able to work as a lawyer for non-Jewish clients, had been working as an adviser to emigrants for some time, which was then a reason he gave [for staying in Germany]: 'I can't leave because I'm helping people to get out.'

Susan Oppenheimer, whose father had been arrested on Kristallnacht

My mother was working on all kinds of things, visas for other countries, and she was working on England, America and [Palestine], and I think also Italy.

Many Jews wanted to move to Palestine in the Middle East, where the Jewish religion had originated. But the area was already the home of many Arabs, and they opposed Jewish settlement. Palestine was at that time controlled by Britain, then still a nation with a large Empire and great influence in the Middle East. Britain at first supported Jewish immigration in Palestine, but then changed its policy and began to restrict it.

Susan Oppenheimer

Above all, [my mother was working] to get my father released. We found out that he was in Dachau concentration camp and there were ways of getting people out of concentration camps at that time. You had to have property to give away, a business to sign away and a visa for another country and all those things my mother was working on.

Thousands of the men arrested on *Kristallnacht* were sent to Dachau, just outside Munich, where the Nazis had built one of the first concentration camps.

Susan Oppenheimer

[When my father] arrived back from Dachau he was a changed man. He had a lot of nice wavy, dark brown hair when he went in and [now] he had grey stubble. They had shaved his head and it came through grey and he was a very angry man. Normally, German men in those days wore hats in the winter and he was walking round without a hat on and I was a bit embarrassed because of the way he looked. People didn't [shave their heads] in those days and I kept saying, 'Oh do put your hat on, Daddy!' And he would say, 'No, I'm not ashamed. They have to be ashamed. This is what they've done to me, let them see.' So he never put his hat on.

Like so many other people, [he] thought Hitler couldn't possibly last. [He thought] he was a madman, he had no idea how to run a country, his policies were ridiculous, and [he] was a temporary thing.

The other thing he said was, 'I will be a refugee wherever I go and I [will] have to start again. I'm nearly 50 and it's difficult for me to start all over again.'

Though some people were reluctant to leave even now, the majority of Jews did want to get out. Inevitably, some decided to do so illegally, without the necessary paperwork.

Barbara Isralowitz, emigrated to Britain illegally with her father in 1938, aged 15

It was decided that my father would go [first] and then apply for a permit for the rest of the family to follow. I by then simply had had enough of the atmosphere in Germany. I felt that my father was abominably treated, I totally identified with him, and I [had] just had enough of it. I wanted to get out. And [my family] felt quite happy to allow me to go with him.

So [after sneaking across the border into Belgium] we went to Antwerp and we took a room over a little pub. And in the daytime we would go together [to] the harbour and my father would ask for the first mate and in the end he ferreted out someone who would be prepared to take us illegally. And he paid for each of us to be smuggled aboard this merchant ship.

One evening we came to the ship and he took us to the engine room, and shut us in. Then once we were on our way he fetched us up and showed us out for a breath of fresh air and we were terribly seasick. And he put us back into the [engine] room. And the whole trip I think took two and a half days.

So then we were [there] when the inspection came – [customs] inspectors – and he warned us we must keep very quiet and everything will be all right. We heard voices and the inspectors came all over the ship but they didn't come to the [engine] room.

Then the captain and the crew went on shore leave, leaving our sailor. And he put us into a rowing boat and rowed us. We were in Greenwich. [He] rowed us to the bank and we just climbed over and we were in the street then. We just walked down the road and there was a tube station and my father knew about tubes, he'd been to England once before. And we asked for a ticket to the Strand. We spoke enough English for that. And we just boarded a tube and we got out at the Strand. And there we were, right in the heart of London.

Between 1933 and 1939, roughly 300,000 Jews – about two thirds of Germany's Jewish population – left the country. 50,000 were officially accepted in Britain, 57,000 in the United States, 53,000 in Palestine, 40,000 in France, and 25,000 in Belgium. Switzerland, Argentina, Brazil, Australia and Canada also accepted significant numbers.

■ ■ ■ ■ ■

He's going to look at my sandwich

As a result of intense pressure from refugee organizations, the British Government did agree to one special rescue plan for thousands of German, Austrian and, later, Czech children. (Unfortunately the same generosity was not extended to their parents.) Refugees under the age of 17 would be allowed into Britain, and foster parents would be found for them, as long as their real parents could pay for their upkeep themselves or find someone else who would agree to do so.

As soon as the plan was announced, thousands of families rushed to register for places and the first children of the 'Kindertransports' ('child transports') left Germany on 1 December 1938.

Hana Bandler, from Prague, aged 15

When the telegram came that I was to come to England, we were given instructions that no valuables, only provisions for the train, and one suitcase were to be taken. So my father went out and bought the largest, lightest case that there was. The suitcase had my number painted on one of the corners.

The prospect of leaving home was daunting, especially for younger children. Many had almost no idea where they were going – Britain was just a place they'd heard about and few knew anything about it or spoke much English.

Bertha Engelhard, from Munich, aged 15

There were scenes at the station. The parents were fainting and the kids were crying and screaming. Some parents pushed their children in when they weren't supposed to go on the transport. Others took them back again because they could not bear to part with them. It was pretty chaotic.

Walter Rechnitzer, from Vienna, aged 12

I went up to my father and put my arms around him and I said, 'I love you so much.' He kissed me and said, 'Try and behave, be a good boy.' I went up to mother and she kissed me and I could see tears in her eyes. As we got on the train, they shut the door, we tried to open the windows and all of a sudden these black uniforms appeared and they pushed our parents back, they weren't allowed to come near us. Father tried to shout something but with all the commotion, we couldn't hear.

Dorothy Oppenheimer

We got into a compartment which was fairly full of children, and the older ones decided that the little ones would go on a luggage rack which was made of netting – they would be more comfortable up there. So we put my little sister up there and she was promptly sick, which was actually very helpful, because the next half hour I was very busy. And my parents said, 'Look after your sister. We must go now and we'll follow you soon. Bye-bye.' And off they went, which was very sensible – and they did follow eventually.

Young Jewish refugees arrive in Britain during one of the Kindertransports

Only a very few of the Kindertransport children were ever reunited with their parents, most of whom became trapped in Germany when international borders were closed at the outbreak of war. The majority of them died in Nazi concentration camps.

Dorothy Oppenheimer

Now, the journey started off with rumours going down the train that soon, when we got to the border, the Nazis would come and inspect our papers and our luggage and if they found anything that we shouldn't have, we might get sent back or there might be trouble.

Maria Siegel

We were allowed to take only ten marks [the German currency] with us and my mother wanted me to have a little bit more, so she put another ten-mark note into a sandwich and wrapped it up. And we got to the border and these Nazis were striding through the railway carriages and I thought, 'He's going to look at my sandwich. I'm sure he's going to look at my sandwich.' Of course, he didn't care two hoots about my sandwich!

Inge Engelhard's passport

Inge Engelhard, from Munich, aged 9

Sometimes it was quite traumatic, because the Nazis would get in and search the luggage and be quite brutal. But the minute you got to Holland, the atmosphere of peace! We'd never had a peaceful atmosphere before and the people were kind and there were ladies there with drinks and cake and making us welcome, and that was beautiful. It was our first taste of freedom ever.

Maria Siegel

And then we chugged on again [through Holland] and that's when I saw my first windmill and I just thought it was so amazing that windmills were real. I just thought they were storybook things and they were absolutely real and I thought, 'I *must* tell my mother.' And that's the second time I realized [I wasn't] going to be seeing her.

Then we got on to the ship in Hook van Holland and it was night-time and when we woke up, we were at Harwich port, and I was so cross because I'd never seen the sea and I was so looking forward [to it].

Then we got on the train to Liverpool Street which I thought was a very funny name – Liver-*pool*? – *Liv*-er-*pool*? – and there we were ushered into rather a dingy hall with bare bulbs rather high up so it wasn't particularly light, and we sat on low school benches and peoples' names were called out and there were all these grown-ups standing in front with this person reading from a list, and nobody called my name and I thought, 'Well what happens now?'

Inge Engelhard

Everything was black and dark, rather smoky. And we just sat there and names were being called out and people collected a child and some of them were crying, didn't want to go. And [there was] a man from the Refugee Committee. He didn't speak German and I thought everybody has to speak German, I thought it was natural, and I was babbling away to him in German and I told him I didn't want to be left to the last. Anyway he bought me a banana and he took me to the station and I was babbling away in German to him and he didn't answer, but put me into a train and said something in this babble language of his to a lady, to look after me no doubt and to put me down at Coventry. Because that's where I was destined to be sent, to Coventry – in *all* ways!

Maria Siegel
And then they called out my name and got the pronunciation a bit wrong. But I realized that it must be me and I leapt up and there was this lady in a lilac-coloured suit [who] struck me as really ancient. She seemed to me a very old lady and she said, 'How do you do?' And I said, 'Yes!'

> By September 1939, when war broke out and borders were closed, almost 10,000 children had reached Britain through the Kindertransport scheme. Other children were not so lucky. On 13 May 1939 a liner called the *St Louis* left Germany bound for Cuba, carrying 930 refugees, including many children. Most of them were on a long waiting list for entry into the United States, and they had been led to believe that they could stay in Cuba until their turn came. But the Cuban Government changed its mind and refused to let the majority of the refugees land. Eventually the *St Louis* turned round and brought them back to Europe. There, France, Holland and Belgium agreed to take in most of them, and Britain took the rest. But a year later Germany invaded France, Holland and Belgium, and in the end fewer than 300 refugees from the *St Louis* survived the War.

How nicely English people live!

Many Kindertransport children arrived in Britain before foster families had been found for them, so in the meantime they were sent to stay in out-of-season holiday camps on the east coast. Unfortunately these were unheated, and that winter was especially severe, so many of the children were extremely cold. But the camps gave them the opportunity to get to know each other and to begin to learn some English. And the camp entertainers at least tried to cheer them up.

Jewish children at a camp in the UK

Gisela Spanglet, stayed at a holiday camp in Dovercourt, Essex, aged 13

He was terribly good with us because he got us all to sing – things like 'Daisy, Daisy' and 'I Like a [Nice] Cup of Tea in the Morning' and 'The Lambeth Walk'. And he kept us busy and got us all to sing. And there was a reluctance to sing anything in English but he was very good, he stood no nonsense, he got everyone to participate.

As they settled in to their new lives, and struggled with the new language, most of the children felt relieved to get out of Germany, even though they missed their parents and often worried about them.

Inge Engelhard, fostered with her brother and sister by a family in Coventry

The beginning was very bewildering. Little things like cornflakes and English breakfasts were very strange to me. But life in England was so leisurely, and there wasn't all this terrible tension that we'd had in Germany and everything that was strange was a nice strangeness. And school was so different, it wasn't so demanding and they did nice things like handicrafts and had a big playground. In the German school, we just had a little yard and we used to walk round and round a bit like prisoners. And the [English] children and the teachers were very kind to me.

Maria Siegel, fostered by a family at Braystead Hall, Sevenoaks, Sussex

It was a bit difficult for poor Miss Williams, later Auntie Estelle, to make conversation with me. I do remember, at one point, she asked me if I wanted to go to the loo. I thought she had asked me to shut the door, and I said, 'Oh yes' and leapt to my feet – and she thought it was nearly too late.

Many of the refugees were very happy with the families that agreed to look after them, and some certainly landed on their feet in terms of creature comforts. Others were less fortunate. Some stayed in households that were much less well off, and some even found that their new English families expected them to act as the hired help. Not all foster families were Jewish, and some children – especially those with more traditional Jewish backgrounds – found this a strain. Other children simply found that the people who had agreed to look after them did not turn out to be as friendly as they seemed at first.

Maria Siegel

Braystead Hall was a splendid place with a circular drive with a fountain in the middle and steps up and as you came in. There was the drawing room on the right and the dining room on the left. Umpteen servants rushing around and a fruit garden and a vegetable garden and a tennis court and waterlily pond. And I thought, 'How nicely English people live!'

Inge Engelhard

I remember at the beginning, we used to go out on a Sunday with them. He had a little car and they took us with [them], but then gradually, we were relegated to the kitchen to eat, which we preferred actually. We weren't part of the family any more – we were the servants. They used to always tease us and say, 'Ah, your people wouldn't take you, we have to.' And in a way, it was true because there weren't enough Jews to take the Jewish children. But, on the other hand, there was such pressure at the beginning of the War and so many mistakes were made, well-meaning mistakes, but it was luck of the draw. There were a lot of children who were very happy and who really landed softly [but] we didn't. On the other hand, we were alive and I think you have to look on the bright side of things. I'm very grateful to them, although we had a very hard time. And I'm very grateful that we weren't separated.

Few of the children who came to Britain as refugees in 1938 or 1939 were old enough to remember much of what life had been like in Germany before Hitler. So some things that British children often took for granted came as a pleasant surprise to most of them.

Susan Oppenheimer, came to Britain in 1938, aged 16, but not part of the Kindertransport. Stayed with English friends of her parents

They took me round London to show me the sights and when we got to Downing Street, there was a huge demonstration: anti-government, down with this and down with that, great banners and shouting. And I was completely bowled over. I said, 'Why aren't they all arrested? Why is nobody shooting?'

John Silbermann, from Berlin, came to Britain on the Kindertransport in 1939, aged 13

Here we would stand at the kerbside waiting to cross where there was a crossing. Suddenly a bobby would arrive from nowhere and he'd just put his hand up and wave us across and smile and [say] 'How are you?' A policeman was the enemy in Germany, [but in Britain] he doesn't carry a gun, he's willing to chat with you. [In Britain] nobody was against you. Some people may not have been your friends, but nobody was *against* you.

Nevertheless, life in Britain wasn't always quite so pleasant. Some British people cared little about what was going on in Germany and a few were suspicious of the refugees simply because they were Germans.

Gerti Seewald, from Wiesbaden, came to Britain on the Kindertransport in 1939, aged 14

This schoolmistress I stayed with was quite unsympathetic as far as I was concerned. She sort of rubbed it in that of course I was a foreigner, I was German, and that people wouldn't particularly like me. So I didn't exactly like her very much.

Barbara Isralowitz

We Jewish refugees had been disowned by our country and we in turn disowned Germany. But English people who've never been rejected by [their] country, they find it very difficult to understand that you mustn't have some loyalty somewhere towards the country where you were born. And the Jewish refugees were very rejecting of Germany at that time.

Though it never reached anything like the proportions that it did in Nazi Germany, anti-Semitism was not completely unknown in Britain and refugees occasionally experienced it. Britain even had its own 'Nazi' Party, the British Union of Fascists, led by Oswald Mosley. Fortunately it had few followers.

What a great power

In March 1939, Hitler broke the agreement he'd made at Munich the year before. He sent his troops further into Czechoslovakia, carving up the country and incorporating more than half of it into Germany. Britain and France stood by while millions more people (including thousands of Jews) became subject to Nazi rule.

Invading German troops enter the castle in the Czech capital city, Prague

Henry Metelmann

I remember looking at the new map, and at school we were always urged on in this way. Now Czechoslovakia was cleaned up, it wasn't sticking out, but Poland was sticking into Germany. And to my way of thinking it was a little bit of a nuisance, a sore thumb. And in one's mind one drew the line across Poland. 'Now if this belongs to Germany too, then what a great power [we'll be]!' And I began to think, 'Well, one day we'll take that lot and good luck to us.'

Six months later Hitler ordered the invasion of Poland. Britain and France finally decided they had given Hitler enough chances, and two days later they declared war.

Margarit Dierksen

I remember being very excited. It was something happening and we saw all these chaps in uniform. Oh yes, but you weren't told that Germany started it. Hitler entered Poland and [it was] 'wonderful'. It was all glorified, the war.

Henry Metelmann

Well Germany had invaded Poland, and to us it was something great. I had no idea what it really meant to the people there, to be invaded by a foreign army, and anyway, to be honest, I didn't care. I thought of the German greatness and I thought, 'Well anyway, the Poles are second rate, and it serves them right.'

My parents were rather quiet about it, and neighbours too, they did not like it, because they remembered the First World War. 'I remember,' [my father] said, 'at first it was all great but then later on things changed.'

■ ■ ■ ■ ■

Britain 1938–1939

1930s The British Government fears that any future war in Europe will probably result in many civilian casualties as a result of heavy bombing. It begins to think about evacuating (removing) children from towns and cities in the event of war.

Summer 1938 Hitler's behaviour means that war with Nazi Germany now seems likely. The Government begins to take active steps to try to protect its civilian population. These include building public bomb shelters, rigging up air-raid sirens and supplying everyone with a gas mask. The Government also draws up detailed plans for evacuating children from built-up areas.

January 1939 Despite the Munich Agreement, the Government continues to plan for a possible evacuation. Surveys are made of all households in the countryside to find out how much space is available. Anyone who has room in their house will have to take in at least one evacuee, if necessary. No checks will be made to ensure that host families are suitable, and children will not be matched with them in advance. Instead, the plan is to move them into the countryside as fast as possible and then use local volunteers to allocate them to new homes. This will inevitably be a fairly haphazard business. It also means that children will have no idea where they are going to end up. Evacuation will be a complete step into the unknown.

February 1939 The British Government begins to issue urban households with 'DIY' bomb shelters for people to set up in their gardens.

Summer 1939 Britain and France have promised to fight Germany if Hitler invades Poland. Hitler appears undeterred and war now seems inevitable. Many families make private arrangements to send their children to stay with friends and relatives in the countryside or abroad.

1 September 1939 In the early hours of the morning German troops pour across the border into Poland. Later in the morning the British Government puts into operation its evacuation scheme. Within 72 hours, around one and a half million children from British towns and cities have found new homes in the countryside.

3 September 1939 At 11.15 am Prime Minister Neville Chamberlain announces on the radio that Britain has declared war on Germany. A few minutes later air-raid sirens are heard in London, though this turns out to be a false alarm. Later in the day France also declares war on Germany, and so do Australia and New Zealand. The Second World War has begun.

What a strange holiday

Britain: 1–3 September 1939

The shape of things to come   64
'Wonder who we'll get?'   67
'You'll do'   72
'We'll make the best of it'   75
A bottle of Tizer   79

The shape of things to come

As people in Britain heard the news about Hitler's conquests of Austria and then Czechoslovakia, there were growing fears about what a war with Germany would mean for civilians.

During the First World War the Germans had dropped bombs from airships and aeroplanes, but they'd had a limited effect. Now Hitler had hundreds of specialized bomber aircraft capable of causing much wider destruction. There was also the prospect of his planes dropping poisonous gas.

Up till now few children in Britain had given much thought to the danger posed by Hitler, but with parents growing more worried by the day, they soon got the picture.

Irene Weller, from Birmingham, aged 12 in 1938

I didn't take much notice of all the war clouds gathering. I can remember seeing on all the posters outside the newsagents all the war news. It was all Poland. And dimly I used to think, 'I wonder why I keep reading all this?' But it really didn't mean anything.

And then they came round and issued us with gas masks, it was quite a frightening experience. Once it was on your face it was very restricting and the smell of the rubber! You could hardly wait to get it off, and you looked absolutely atrocious. And I think that was the night it really came home to us all. This was the shape of things to come.

Very young children were given special red and blue 'Mickey Mouse' gas masks, which were supposed to look a bit like the cartoon character to make them more appealing. Babies were placed inside larger contraptions that had to be operated with a bellows pump.

A gas mask specially made for babies

Joanna Rogers, from Croydon, south London, aged 8 in 1938

My parents talked about it a lot at home. And as a family we talked quite a lot about it. I remember Mother stocking up with food. We had a siren put on that was tested and this was really quite near to us. And we had a funny little thing at the end of the road, a square thing on a stick, it was about a foot square. It was painted green that we were told would go yellow in the event of a gas attack. And the top of the letterbox near us was painted green too. That would also go yellow in the event of a gas attack. That was the thing that worried us.

Gas-detecting paint, which changed colour when it came into contact with gas, was painted on the top of red Post Office pillar boxes and in other prominent places.

Some time during that year before the War we were issued with gas masks that we found we could make rude noises with. If you blew out fast they'd vibrate along the sides of them and we could make rude noises. [ARP] wardens used to go round with whistles blowing for the practice blackouts. Now that, as far as I can remember, was the only thing that did frighten me and I felt particularly that one chink of light and a bomb would be raining down on us. My mother made blackout curtains, I can remember that. And I felt one chink of light and it would be it.

> ARP (Air Raid Precautions) wardens were local volunteers whose job was to make sure everyone knew what to do in an air raid. Blackouts – which officially began on 1 September 1939 – were a way to make things more difficult for enemy bombers. All lights were either extinguished or covered up so that cities were not so easy to spot at night from the air. All civilians were responsible for making sure that no light could be seen from outside their houses.

British schoolchildren practising wearing gas masks

By September 1939 about one and a half million children had registered for the Government's evacuation scheme, which was organized through their schools. This was fewer than expected, but many parents were reluctant to send their children to stay with complete strangers. Those who had friends or relations in the countryside often preferred to make private arrangements. Others chose to keep their family all together at home, despite the risk of bombing.

Muriel Shean, from Woolwich, south London, aged 12 in 1939

I think our parents had to go to the school and they were given a little chat about it and told what we should take with us, and that after we'd arrived a blackboard would be put outside the school in the evening to tell them where we'd gone. We were quite excited and looking forward to it really because it sounded interesting to go and live in the country.

Irene Weller

At school it was all 'Are you going or are you going to stay?' And then by this time my mother was really upset. And tears was rolling down her face. Meantime everything had to be ready because we didn't know which day we'd be going.

'Wonder who we'll get?'

In the end the go-ahead for the evacuation was given on the last day of August, when German troop movements on the Polish border made it obvious that an invasion was imminent. On the following morning – Friday 1 September – hundreds of thousands of children set off for school, not knowing where they would be by evening. There they lined up in classes while teachers made sure they were ready.

Irene Weller

There we were with our best coat – well, the only coat we'd got, probably – and our shoes very well polished. I remember my mother saying, 'We must get your shoes polished well because that's very important.' A label was put round our necks with a bit of string with our name and our home address on. Everybody was standing there with a label around their neck. My younger brother was very, very tearful. And we just looked dumbfounded really. I don't know whether I had any special thoughts about it. I suppose I might have thought, 'Well, I shan't get lost anyway.'

Evacuees waiting for a train. The parcels contain gas masks

Muriel Shean

We weren't allowed to take too much, just a few clothes. And we had to wear a mac, strong shoes, that sort of thing. But we didn't take a lot of toys or anything. There wouldn't have been room.

Dennis Hayden, from Portsmouth, aged 7

I can remember having a little brown attaché case with a little clip on it. Probably ten-a-penny in Woolworth's at the time. Then the [gas mask] – white box, white tape. And eventually a big label tied on us. It seemed like you were a parcel being bundled off somewhere and hopefully you would arrive at the destination. But you didn't know where you were going. All it said was where you had come from.

Anxious parents were waiting outside the schools, but to prevent overcrowding on the station platforms, they were not allowed to come any further and were told to return home. Then teachers took the children on foot or by bus to the nearest train station.

Irene Weller

This to me was the worst day of the whole War. The teachers came and they told the mothers that they must say their goodbyes. And eventually there was quite a number of weeping women all just going home. And we were all assembled outside the school, all in lines. Some of the children were crying. But most of them were all chattering. At this point we didn't know where we were going and neither did the mothers.

To walk up the road we'd got to pass my mother's house anyway. And I knew she'd be on the step. I can remember all the ladies being all there on the front doorsteps outside their houses all the way up. And eventually after having checked everything – had you got a clean hankie? – we all piled over the road. And I'd got a brother either side of me. One was eleven and one was nine.

I said, 'Don't look round whatever you do, because I know that Mum will be looking.' We just looked straight ahead. And when we got right past her I looked at the two lads and the tears were just falling down our faces.

Evacuees on their way to a London station

At mainline stations, people trying to get to work that day found that normal services had been suspended for 72 hours because so many trains were needed for the evacuation.

Joan Chantrelle, from Woodford, east London, aged 13

The train came and we climbed in. I was a bit bewildered. I was upset because my young sister was crying so I had to be the stiff upper lip. The platform seemed completely crammed with children. The station was absolutely packed. I don't remember anybody actually shepherding us or looking after things. I just remember us climbing on to the train and it being absolutely packed, children standing.

The luggage was put on racks but a lot of it was just sort of on laps. It was very, very crammed and crowded, and crying is the thing I remember more than anything, children crying. I wanted to cry desperately but I just daren't because of Naomi. I'd just got to have this stiff upper lip. And I said we were really only on holiday. She must have thought, 'What a strange holiday.'

Irene Weller

Of course a train ride to us then was the height of excitement. And we were so thrilled about getting on this train. We forgot all our fears for a bit. The plan was to stick together. And after the train had started – and of course it was all steam so that was excitement when it started to puff out – you couldn't see anything except clouds of steam.

Gwendoline Watts, from Birmingham, aged 13

I felt sorry at having to say goodbye to my mother, but once she was out of sight all the girls began to line up. And I can remember sitting in the carriage talking with the other girls. Because we'd heard by then that we were going to foster people and we were all saying, 'Wonder who we'll get?' and 'Wonder where the boys are going from the boys' school?'

Ronald McGill, from Vauxhall, south London, aged 9

We whizzed under a funny old archway at Clapham Junction. And when we went under there we could see people lined up above it all waving to us and that cheered us up no end. And then we were into Putney and then we saw fields, the commons. And then we went out through Richmond across the Thames and you know we were in the countryside. And it wasn't long before we saw cows and cattle. No, we were thrilled – it was a tremendous adventure for us.

Evacuees waving from their crowded train

Some children went only a few miles to villages just outside their home towns. Others went on much longer journeys, some of them travelling halfway across the country before their teachers told them it was time to get off.

'You'll do'

On arrival at their various destinations, children were taken to school halls, hotels and other temporary 'reception centres'. Then the process of allocating them to host families began. Volunteers called 'billeting officers' supervised while local people came along to collect their evacuees. They had been told how many children they were supposed to take (depending on how much room they had), but it was up to them to come and pick the children themselves. No attempt had been made to make suitable matches, it was simply a matter of 'first come, first served'. For some children this selection process was relatively quick. For others it proved to be an ordeal.

Gwendoline Watts, evacuated from Birmingham to Ashby-de-la-Zouch in Leicestershire

We were all ushered into the ballroom at the Queen's Hotel and we had to gather into our classes. And officials were there and they had long lists of names, and we were just called forward and given to the person who took us away. And my name was called with another girl, Barbara, and fortunately we got on well together. And this lady said, 'Come with me.' And I ventured up enough courage to say, 'Where are we going?' And she said 'Well, you're two very lucky girls. You're going to a sweetshop.' Oh, living in a sweetshop! Paradise!

Ronald McGill, evacuated from London to Reading

We were just put off at Reading, but the train went on. And we were all taken into a big school, and then we were given a meal.

They said that people would be coming into the hall for us, and would we all just line up along the side. And people came in, and they walked down the line and I was taken by local council people. We were just earmarked: 'We wanted a boy and a girl. You'll do.' *Boomp* – out. They probably picked the ones that were better dressed. Mum had made sure that we were wearing nice clothes.

Joan Chantrelle, evacuated with her sister Naomi from London to Ongar, Essex

They walked around as if we were cattle. They were looking at us, you know, eyeing us up and down and wandering back and forth. And various women came and collected the children. Then slowly but surely the hall became deserted and Naomi and I were still standing there. It turned out to be the billeting officer we went with.

Evacuees get a meal before they are allocated to foster familes

Irene Weller, evacuated with her two younger brothers from Birmingham to Stratford

At the finish it must have been about eight o'clock and we were the only three left. And I thought, 'Golly, it's getting dark and what's going to happen to us?' But I thought as long as the teachers are still with us they'll look after us.

But my younger brother kept saying, 'I want to go back home.' And by this time they were starting to cry a little bit.

Eventually my teacher Miss Richards she said, 'Now come along, Irene. We're going to take you to a very nice place. But I'm afraid that you will have to split from your two brothers because that's the way things are.'

It was dreadful really. By now they were openly crying and I was sobbing. But I just had to go. And I remember going in a car because I think I'd only ever had two car rides in my life before that. It seemed hours to me. But we came to this lovely bungalow, and we knocked on the door and the door opened. And a great big black dog put his face right in front of mine and his paws on my shoulder. And I thought, 'Right, this is it now, this is the end of everything.' Because I was scared of dogs. But he was to become my pal. And then a grey-haired lady came to the door and she said, 'Well, come in. I didn't *want* you, but come in.'

May George, evacuated from Manchester to Derbyshire, aged 12
I can remember this Lucy in the village. She had a little shop up at the top of the village, a little hut. 'Oh dear,' she said, 'Three of you. I really don't know who will take three of you.' So I think we were the last ones standing in the school. So Lucy said, 'Now, I wonder if Mrs Sharples will have you. Come on.' So we walked right up to the top of the village from the school. She knocked on the door. 'Mrs Sharples, I've brought you your evacuees.'

'Come in! Come in!' Oh, from then on it was absolute kindness itself: 'Come in!'

'We'll make the best of it'

By the time they reached their new homes, many evacuees were exhausted, though most still managed to register some first impressions. Many of them were from poorer backgrounds and some were struck by the size of the houses they were taken to, and the luxury they found inside. On the other hand, some evacuees were dismayed to find themselves in farmhouses with no electricity or running water. Experiences varied greatly.

Joan Chantrelle

We then went to their house, which was a lovely detached house with an orchard and a tennis court. Although we came from quite a nice little house, it was lino on the floor and nothing really comfortable about it, but this was plush carpets.

Irene Weller

It was the first time I'd ever been in a bungalow. I thought I was in film-star land to be honest. If my mother had been there I should have thought I was in heaven – but of course, she wasn't.

These children were evacuated to a farm in Devon.
They are clambering up to look at some horses

Margaret Butler, evacuated to a farm in Zeals, Wiltshire

You had to go out into the yard to the toilet which was bitterly cold. They didn't have a tap in the kitchen so there was no hot water anywhere. In the morning you had to use a washbasin and a jug. There was no electricity. It was just oil lamps.

Ronald McGill

It was a very fine house, very classy. And we were handed over to the lady who was ... I don't know if she was a maid but she was [the] person we met. She got us ready for meals and took us down. We hardly really saw the husband and wife that took us. I soiled my trousers and I didn't know where to put them. So I put them in a rack in the front door. It was his umbrella rack. And from that moment he hated the sight of me.

Gwendoline Watts

It was a café-cum-sweet shop, all the sweets on one side. There was a young lady, her name was Cathy and she was the maid. And the owner was in the back room – this little old lady.

We went up these rickety stairs to the bedroom. Big old-fashioned bedstead and massive wardrobes. And Cathy had to light the candles because it was dark. And she said, 'This is your room, you hang your clothes up there. And then you can come down and have some tea.' And Cathy was very nice and very friendly but we weren't sure of the old lady.

So we two schoolgirls went down and we were tired by this time. And there was a plate for Barbara and a plate for me and one tomato on the plate, and a pot of tea. And that was our tea, a tomato and bread and butter. Oh we scoffed that, we were so hungry. And Cathy said, 'When you finish come into the shop.' So we went in and she gave us a few sweets. 'But don't let the old lady see.'

Joanna Rogers, evacuated from London to Brighton

She was a very quiet little lady but we led her a merry dance. She'd obviously never had any children and the two of us together, I think we were rather naughty. We told her we always had foam baths and the poor woman went out next day and bought us foam for our baths.

Joan Chantrelle

The woman showed us up to our room, which was a beautiful room with little chintzy curtains – a real country house. One particular window you could see right across the hills and the countryside, and I thought how lovely this was. And I remember waking in the morning to the birds – which I don't think I'd ever done before – and thought it was really idyllic. And I think the very first morning we were there she brought me a cup of tea in bed.

I was quite happy at this time. Not so Naomi. She wasn't happy at all and she kept on, 'Mummy, mummy, mummy.'

Hundreds of thousands of Britain's children woke up that morning to find themselves in a strange house. Many spent a part of the day tracking down a pen and some paper to write to their parents to tell them where they were. Those who felt homesick or nervous had no choice but to put a brave face on it.

Irene Weller

I got up the next day. And [the lady] says, 'Come along then. We'll make the best of it. We'll see whether we can find your two brothers.' And she took me shopping. And it was a fish shop. And I looked across the counter and there were my two brothers. We ran to each other as though we hadn't seen each other for years.

It transpired that the bungalow that I was in was at the end of a row and they were next door. Of course when we found out we were delighted. And they had found a lovely family. The only thing I didn't like was that she'd got a visiting granddaughter. She was only five and she was quite a tough little soul. And she said if [my brothers] didn't behave she was going to roll up her sleeves. She was only five, she was named Monica and she said she would 'paste' them. That was her words. She was going to give them 'a good pasting'. And my brother, he was frightened out of his life at this Monica.

■ ■ ■ ■ ■

A bottle of Tizer

Two days after the evacuation began, on the morning of Sunday, 3 September, households across the country tuned into BBC radio for an important announcement from the Prime Minister. At 11.15 am Neville Chamberlain broadcast his message from Downing Street:

'This morning the British Ambassador in Berlin handed the German Government a final note stating that, unless we hear from them by 11 o'clock that they were prepared at once to withdraw their troops from Poland, a state of war would exist between us. I have to tell you now that no such undertaking has been received, and that consequently this country is at war with Germany.'

Irene Weller

I can remember everyone with a radio they would listen because I think the Prime Minister was going to receive a message or something. And of course I was sat down in this room while the radio was on and I was praying the War wouldn't start, but of course it did. And [the lady] said: 'Well, you're going to be with me now for some time.'

Joan Chantrelle

I can remember the wireless being on and Mrs Spearman sort of shushing everybody, and hearing the War declared. And the very first thing that Mrs Spearman said to me was, 'Here you are, dear. Go and buy a bottle of Tizer.' It sounds such a strange thing to say but this is what she said. And just a little way along the road was a little general store. Whether she wanted to get us out of the way because they wanted to talk, I don't know, but I went off to this little shop – never ever had a bottle of Tizer in my life. And I knew that war had broken out but I didn't think, 'Oh goodness, isn't this terrible.' It just meant nothing. I'd got the bottle of Tizer and that was marvellous.

Gwendoline Watts

We were sitting in this little sitting room and the old lady came in and took the cover off the radio and turned it on. And she said, 'Now you must listen to this.' And so we listened and it was the Prime Minister making the announcement.

So we listened and the old lady said, 'Now we've got to make sure about the blackouts.' And she made us help her, we had to climb up and fix the blackout curtains around the windows.

This was war now, war had actually started, and it was as if we were on the brink of something and we didn't know what it was.

■■■■■

Europe 1939–1940

September 1939–April 1940 Germany conquers Poland within four weeks. After that there is an unexpected lull in the war. Britain sends its army to France to help the French in case of a German invasion, but the Allies are not yet ready to launch an attack against Germany, and they can do nothing about the German occupation of Poland. Hitler also bides his time and does not bomb British cities. In Britain, where nothing seems to be happening, the period becomes known as the 'Phoney War'. Some people call it the 'Bore War'. As the months pass, and danger fails to materialize, many evacuees return to their homes.

9 April 1940 After seven months, the 'Phoney War' comes to an abrupt end when the Germans swiftly invade both Denmark and Norway.

10 May 1940 In another surprise attack, Germany sends its armies pouring westwards into Holland, Belgium and Luxembourg. That evening, Neville Chamberlain resigns as British Prime Minister and is replaced by Winston Churchill.

14 May 1940 German troops now sweep around and behind the Allied forces defending France. In doing so, they encircle almost 400,000 Allied soldiers, who become trapped against the English Channel near the town of Dunkirk. The Allies face military disaster.

27 May–4 June 1940 More than 300,000 British, French and Belgian troops are successfully evacuated from the beaches of Dunkirk by an armada of ships and boats sent from Britain. Although the rescue is hailed as a great success by many people in Britain, the whole episode is really a catastrophic defeat that leaves most of Western Europe in Hitler's hands.

No-man's-land

Britain: September 1939–May 1940

A whole sausage 84

A different world 88

'Can I come home, please?' 91

I wonder if the war's over 93

A little seaside town 95

A whole sausage

Air-raid sirens had sounded in London only minutes after war was declared, but that had soon turned out to be a false alarm. In the weeks and months that followed, the air raids did not come, and after all the panic of those first days of September, life in Britain soon began to settle back down into a kind of routine.

Sylvia Parkes, not yet evacuated from Margate, Kent, aged 12

It was like living in no-man's-land. You had all the grown-ups talking about the war and the effect it was going to have. But as a child your life seemed to go on very much as usual with certain exceptions, inasmuch that you had things like air-raid drill which you'd never had before. And you chased off to the shelter as soon as the bell rang – the quicker the better in order that you sort of broke the record and did it quicker this time than the last.

We all collected cartoons and funny little bits out of the newspapers to put in a big scrap book to take to read in the shelter. And we all carried our gas masks in our little cardboard box with the snazziest cover we could find, and everybody sort of vied with each other to get the best cover they could. And it was very handy to keep your comb in and little bits and pieces like that.

Within weeks of the outbreak of war, many people in Britain had stopped carrying their gas mask with them. After a few months hardly anybody did. (Though some children still carried the box!)

Since no one seemed to be in terrible danger from bombing, thousands of evacuees soon began to drift back home. For those who remained, the War soon receded into the background. More pressing than Hitler was the problem of living with a new family whose way of life – and especially their diet – was not always what they were used to.

Joan Chantrelle, evacuee in Ongar, Essex

I can remember sitting at a table and having napkins which we didn't have at home. And I wasn't sure what to do. I remember feeling a little uncomfortable because although we were poor we'd been brought up to be correct in everything we did.

Irene Weller, evacuee living next door to her two younger brothers in Stratford, aged 13

[The food] was different. Because of necessity my mother [used to] have to make a little go a long way, and it would perhaps turn up the next day in a different disguise, which was commonplace in those days. And when we had sausages at home we'd only have a third of a sausage, which we always saved till last. [But] at Mrs Paget's I was allowed to have a whole sausage to myself, which I couldn't wait to tell my brothers about.

'You'll never guess what I've had today, *never*,' I said.

And they never did guess that I'd had a whole sausage because such things were beyond our wildest dreams.

During the War, supplies of food imported to Britain from abroad were limited because shipping space was needed for military equipment. As a result, the Government introduced 'rationing' in 1940. All households were issued with ration books containing coupons that could be exchanged for a small amount of each rationed food. Of course, people bent the rules whenever they could, and extra food was sometimes obtainable illegally. Because they lived in the country – on or near farms – many evacuees had more to eat than children who stayed at home.

A young evacuee helps with the harvest

Bacon, butter and sugar were the first foods to be rationed, in January 1940. Gradually, others followed, including meat, tea, jam, margarine, syrup, treacle, milk, dried fruit and rice. Chocolate and sweets went on the ration in July 1942. Soap, clothes and petrol were also rationed, but bread and vegetables were not. Rationing continued in Britain until 1954, nine years after the end of the War.

Sylvia Parkes, evacuated with her 7-year-old brother Bob from Margate to Staffordshire in 1940

We were all rationed to so much meat and so much butter and this, that and the other. But I know we did have *cake*. And Auntie Nancy had this habit of putting the plate so the cake she particularly wanted was facing her because she thought that you never turn things round, you know, you should take the one from nearest. She was very much a stickler for manners and behaviour and we had to do this, that and the other thing and woe betide you if you didn't.

I remember one teatime she went out of the room for something and [my brother] turned the plate round so that the cake that she would have had was on our side of the plate, and one that was not half as interesting was on her side. And I can still see her now. She automatically went to reach for this cake that she thought was going to be there. And it wasn't. And she sort of sat there with her hand in mid-air. She couldn't do a thing about it. She just had to carry on and take the one that was facing her.

And I shall never forget it because Bob sat there with his face as deadpan as anything.

Irene Weller

Every afternoon when they went back [to their house], [my brothers were given] bread and strawberry jam – *every* afternoon. They were very partial to a tomato because my mother had always had them. And they used to say, 'I wonder when ever we're going to have a tomato? I do hope it's this afternoon.' And of course it never was. Anyway, one afternoon she said to them, 'I've got a surprise for you boys. You are not having strawberry jam.' And they could hardly wait for the tomato. 'No, you're having *blackcurrant* jam.'

They were so bitterly disappointed that when she went out of the room they put the bread and jam behind the picture on the wall. When they met me later on they told me what they'd done, and I died a thousand deaths. But I thought, 'Well, we've made our little mark on Stratford.'

A different world

Until they were evacuated, some children had scarcely set foot outside the cities where they'd been born. For them, living in the country was an eye-opening experience, even if the war itself was not.

Ronald McGill, evacuated a second time to Reading, later in the War

The countryside stretched away and I'd never really been on a farm before in my life. I'd only ever fished in ponds on Clapham Common and the local boys took me on their fishing expeditions. I had minnows and jars and pots all over the place. Sticklebacks. There was a famous pumping station where we used to catch perch and tench and things like that. Bream. And they used to take me across some old marshlands there and I learnt [about] lapwings and all different types of birds. I'd never had an egg collection. I'd only ever collected snails and caterpillars in Lambeth. It was a different world.

Dennis Hayden, evacuated from Portsmouth to the New Forest, Hampshire, aged 7

[I remember] the New Forest ponies coming into the garden, eating everything – looking out of the window and suddenly seeing horses in the garden, which being a town dweller, not even knowing these things existed except to pull carts around, was absolutely amazing.

Sylvia Bell, evacuated from Surbiton, just outside London, to Yorkshire

I can remember [the local children] said, 'You come from where the streets are paved with gold?' And they obviously thought London was another world. And of course we were called Cockneys because we had south of England accents – not Cockney accents but they called us Cockney. And we couldn't understand all the "Ee bah gooms'. But I think we got on well with the other children apart from obvious teasing about our accents and where we came from.

Evacuated children play beside a haystack in Devon

Edward Butt, evacuated from East London to Chipping Norton, aged 9

Chipping Norton had two cinemas. And such was the quality of the projectors that the thing broke down. Well, it took a little while to keep us in order, but one boy got up and he sang a song. And we learnt this song, and that song kept us occupied for half an hour. And it was a very old London song: 'We are some of the West Ham boys...' And us evacuees adopted that song as our sort of anthem. And if we felt a bit important or wanted to assert ourselves we would sing this.

When term-time began, the teachers who had organized the evacuation and come along with the evacuees were now expected to run classes for them. However, space in village schools was limited, and it was often only possible for evacuees to spend a few hours a week in a classroom.

Lessons for evacuees were sometimes held outside

Sylvia Parkes

We didn't have proper lessons. We'd go for a ramble and places of interest, all the places our form master thought we ought to go to. He and his wife took the lot of us. And we used to take sandwiches and have picnics on the common, and play games and cowboys and Indians and heaven knows what. And so really it was more or less a long holiday. I think we learnt a certain amount. But we certainly didn't learn any lessons.

■ ■ ■ ■ ■

'Can I come home, please?'

Many children suffered from homesickness and wrote letters begging their parents to let them come home. As time passed more parents gave in – after all, the cities were not being bombed and nothing at all seemed to be happening. But the Government advised parents to tell their children to stay put, and some evacuees remained in the countryside for the whole six years of the War. The most they could hope for was an occasional visit from their parents at weekends or, if they were very lucky, a brief return home at Christmas.

Gwendoline Watts, living in a sweetshop with her friend Barbara
[My friend] Barbara began to get homesick. So one day a man and lady walked into the café and it was Barbara's mother and father and they'd come to take her home. And I said, 'Can I come home too, please?' And they said, 'Oh, no, no, you can't go.' So I was stuck there on my own.

The old lady wasn't very much aware of what was going on so Cathy said to her, 'Can I take Gwen to my home for tea on Sunday?' Cathy was the maid in the house and she had Sundays off.

So she took me up to her house, which was a council house in Ashby. She had three or four brothers and sisters and I let my hair down there because I was one of the children and I had someone to play with. And massive meals in front of me, and I really tucked into those meals. We were literally starved in that house, in the [sweetshop]. We didn't say anything, we just thought this was the way it was supposed to be until Cathy said, 'You must come home and have a meal with us. I'll fill you up.'

And this became a routine. Every day of the week I looked forward to Sunday to go to a house, a normal house and people. Because the old lady just hobbled about on her stick and she didn't know we were there.

The Government made its advice to parents of evacuees clear in posters like these

Joan Chantrelle

We went home for Christmas. And the thing that impressed me most of all was the journey because it was in the blackout. All the station[s] were blacked out and the trains were blacked out apart from tiny little dots of light. The train came and we got on, we were the only ones in the carriage, and it was very dark. And every time we came to a station I peered to see the name because I was terrified that we'd not get out at the right station. But we did, and my mother met us and that was absolutely glorious. We walked down Snakes Lane, a long, long lane home. All the houses were pitch black because the blackouts were up, and it really [was] black, black dark.

> During the blackout, streetlights were not lit. No lights were permitted in trains or buses, and car headlights also had to be masked. A poll taken in January 1940 revealed that one person in five had had some kind of accident as a result of the blackout.

And I remember going home and thinking how lovely this was. We hadn't seen it for what seemed years and it was a marvellous feeling. And it was Christmas and of course everywhere was the festive spirit and although the shops were blacked out when it was dark there was a marvellous atmosphere. I always remember the grocers because you know they shovelled out the sultanas, and the broken biscuits we used to buy – and that was great. And we bought all the stuff for Christmas and came home. Mother bought a little Christmas tree and I decorated it with silver paper from cigarette packets because we couldn't have afforded decorations. And it was all just marvellous.

I wonder if the war's over

In many cases, evacuees had to get used to more than one new home. Host families sometimes complained to the authorities about not having enough space, or simply said that they couldn't get on with the children they'd got. As a result, some evacuees ended up being moved from one household to another, sometimes several times.

Joan Chantrelle, moved from family to family several times

I was very unhappy being pushed around all the time. There was never any explanation and there was this feeling of 'Well, what have we got to move again for?' And I thought 'Well, why *are* we evacuated?'

There wasn't any bombing. We were going through all these traumas when we could have been at home nicely with mother and father. Most of our schoolmates were at home.

I used to pray like mad in bed. [At home] I could never pray, all I could say was 'Bless Mummy, bless Daddy, bless the cat…' I couldn't formulate a prayer. But I remember being evacuated [and] praying, praying, praying at night-time to get out of this awful thing.

Gwendoline Watts

And I can remember a lady came to the [sweet] shop and she sent for me and she said, 'You're being moved. You're going to a nice house just by the school. Pack your things.'

And this was a youngish man and lady and they had a little daughter about four years of age. And I hated them. Everyone thought they were so kind and they weren't. The little girl, I think her name was Pauline but I know she became 'It'. And I became that girl's nursemaid. They wouldn't let me do my homework because I had to sit with this child. I had to get up before them in the morning to get the child up and give it its breakfast. I had to rush home in the lunchtime from the school across the way, get the lunch on the go, give the child its lunch. And she was a little terror. And she would break things and I would be blamed for the breakage because they said, '*Pauline* wouldn't do a thing like that.'

My mother would send me a shilling every week. So I started putting this shilling away. Another week, another shilling.

So one day, I was walking down Market Street and the bus stopped. I just happened to look at the destination board and it said Birmingham. And I hopped on.

My mother and father didn't know I was coming, I didn't know what sort of a reception I would get but I knew I had to get away from there. My mother came to the door and she said, 'What are you doing here?'

I said, 'I've come home.'

She sat me down, I had a cup of tea and I told her. Then she said, 'Well, you should have come home before.'

And I can remember saying, 'People don't like evacuees, do they, Mum?'

Plenty of people did *like evacuees, and treated them well, but there were some who didn't and quite a few children ended up running away. (Not all were welcomed with understanding by their parents, and in some cases they were sent straight back.) On the whole, the more anxious the evacuees were to get home, the more the War seemed to drag on.*

Irene Weller

I remember coming down one morning [and] I thought, 'Oh, I wonder if the War's over today.' So I remember going to the front door and picking the newspaper up. I thought, 'Oh, it's bound to be on the front page.' But of course it wasn't.

And I remember Mrs Paget saying, 'You mustn't read at the table.' Well I was nowhere *near* the table. And I said, 'Well, I wanted to see whether the War was over.'

And she said, 'You silly little child. I'd have told you.' And I thought, 'Oh well, perhaps it'll be over tomorrow.'

But of course it wasn't.

A little seaside town

Far from being over, the War soon took a decisive turn for the worse when on 10 May 1940 Hitler sent his armies pouring westwards towards Holland, Belgium and France. It was a devastating move that took everybody by surprise, but although Holland fell quickly and Belgium looked sure to follow, French and British forces stood between the Germans and France itself, and most people expected them to stand firm.

As German soldiers approached Belgium's capital Brussels, thousands of civilians fled towards France where they thought they'd be safe. They included a number of German Jewish refugees who had emigrated to Belgium to escape the Nazis.

Elisabeth Lukas, German Jewish girl, lived in Belgium since 1933 when she emigrated with her family and her frog, aged 17

On 14 May people started leaving Brussels because obviously the news was bad and the Germans were getting closer. By that time Holland had already surrendered. My mother, brother and I decided to go to France with everybody else. It had never occurred to anybody that France could not resist.

We left by train [and] got as far as Tournai, very near the French border. We walked towards the border on roads that were crowded, many cars loaded up to the top. And about three or four miles from the border it was completely at a standstill, but we were walking.

It was a very hot day. It was the beautiful month of May. My mother was a very elegant woman and had no shoes with flat heels, and [she was] walking along the dusty roads in May 1940 on high heels. And we saw Tournai being bombed. And it was very, very spectacular.

When we got [to the border] we were asked to show our identity papers. And we had cards saying, 'German', and we were turned back. And this was really quite a nightmare. So we started walking back on this road, passing all the cars waiting to get into France. People said, 'Why are you coming back? Is the border closed?' And the answer was always, 'No, the border isn't closed.' 'Why are you coming back, then?' Well, you couldn't say, 'Because we're *Germans*.' It was a real nightmare. From car to car the same question, and there was no answer.

Then we stopped at a little roadside café which had run out of everything. We had a glass of water and were sitting there. They had the radio on and they were listening to the French broadcast, and this was the first time that we realized that things were going very badly for France. France was in danger.

A family of refugees in a ruined town in Belgium, May 1940

Within a fortnight Belgium had surrendered and the German army had swept around the Allied armies and into France itself. British, French and Belgian forces found themselves completely encircled and pinned against the sea. A desperate rescue operation from the beaches of Dunkirk saved over 300,000 troops – two-thirds of them British – but they had to leave all their weapons and equipment behind.

Elisabeth Lukas

We ended up at a little seaside town [on the coast], just next to Dunkirk, and we got stuck there. It was absolutely full of refugees. And one day we came across some Belgian soldiers who were coming back and [one of them] was wearing carpet slippers. He must have had very sore feet and discarded his boots. And he said as far as he was concerned the War was finished.

We didn't know that the British were getting out. We knew nothing, only that the bombing came closer and closer. There was only one thing to do – go back to Brussels. And we started walking. The road was littered with British [equipment] and clothes and uniforms and dead horses.

Although the rescue of troops at Dunkirk was talked about in England as a 'miracle', this could not hide the fact that it was also a humiliating withdrawal that meant the collapse of Allied defences in the West. Three weeks later, France surrendered. Hitler now had almost complete control of Europe.

Civilians in Holland, Belgium and France would have to endure years of occupation, and thousands of Jews who had escaped Nazi Germany in the 1930s once again found themselves living under Nazi rule.

Britain was now the only country in Europe still at war with Hitler and not yet occupied, but its army was in tatters and German forces were building up across the Channel. The War wasn't 'phoney' any more.

■ ■ ■ ■ ■

The Polish ghettos 1939–1941

1930s There are about three million Jews living in Poland – ten per cent of the population and more than a third of all the Jews in Europe. Most are much more traditional in their religion and way of life than the Jews of western Europe. There is a long history of anti-Semitism in Poland, and unlike western Jews, who tend to mix with their Christian neighbours, most Polish Jews stick together in their own villages or areas of towns and cities. (These areas are known as 'quarters' or 'ghettos'.)

1 September 1939 Germany invades Poland, which collapses in only a few weeks. Half of Poland is occupied by Germany and half by the Soviet Union (whose leader, Josef Stalin, has made a deal with Hitler to split Poland between them). Many Poles are murdered and others dragged off to labour camps. In most cases it is Polish Jews who come in for the worst treatment.

8 October 1939 In a town called Piotrkow the Nazis force all Jews not already living in the Jewish quarter to move into it. Jews from surrounding villages are also forced to move there. This pattern is soon repeated in scores of towns and cities all over German-occupied Poland. Jews are 'concentrated' into existing Jewish ghettos, and then confined there – sometimes behind specially built walls and fences. These closed ghettos become dreadfully overcrowded.

November–December 1939 Jews in German-occupied Poland are forced to wear armbands and badges bearing the Jewish Star of David symbol.

May–June 1940 The Germans invade Denmark, Norway, Belgium, Luxembourg, Holland and France, bringing half a million more Jews under Nazi rule. However, there are few existing Jewish quarters in these countries, and the Nazis do not try to confine Jews to particular areas. Meanwhile, in Poland, the Nazis seal off more than 160,000 Jews in a ghetto in Lodz, the country's second largest city.

November 1940 Hungary, Romania and Slovakia form an alliance with Germany. In Poland's capital, Warsaw, around 350,000 Jews are enclosed inside a ghetto.

1940–1941 The Nazis force Jews in ghettos to set up their own governing councils and run the ghettos as separate 'towns within towns'. However, the Nazis exploit the Jews inside by forcing them to work for German-owned factories. They also begin to limit their food supply. Conditions inside the ghettos get worse and worse.

Closed in

Poland: 1939–1941

When the Germans came   102
From house to house   104
Decrees went up   106
The gates were closed   109
Its own organization   112
People used to fight for a potato   116

When the Germans came

The German invasion of Poland on 1 September 1939 was quick and decisive. Dive-bombers screamed down on Warsaw, devastating the Polish capital, while hundreds of fast-moving tanks and thousands of troops poured across the border. This was something very different from the slow-moving trench warfare of the First World War. This was 'blitzkrieg' ('lightning war'), and the world had never seen anything like it. Within weeks, the Polish army was crushed. For many Polish people, but especially for Jews, life would never be the same again.

Polish people marched away by a German soldier after the invasion of Poland

Barbara Stimler, Alexandrow Kujawski, Poland, aged 12 in 1939
I had a very, very good childhood. What's stuck in my memory mostly is Yom Kippur [an important Jewish holiday] when my parents used to sit all day long in the synagogue and I used to have some friends

around and we used to put lipsticks on and put my mother's clothes and shoes on. And that was my best time, that time.

Now when the Germans came everything was spoilt for me. By eight o'clock bombs were already flying. It didn't need many bombs to fall on our little town – we didn't have big houses. Unfortunately we quickly ran into the cellar and the bomb hit us, hit our house, just the corner of the house, and the next-door people got all killed.

Edyta Klein, Warsaw, aged 10
We lived very near the zoo – and they had artillery set up in the zoo – and you saw for a couple of days wild animals, you know – tigers and monkeys and so on – on the streets.

Janina Dawidowicz, Warsaw, aged 9
The air raids were absolutely terrifying, they were the most terrifying thing I'd experienced until then. A great part of the town was destroyed. We ended up living in a cellar together with everybody else, and our house was hit several times. There were a lot of casualties.

Tauba Biber, Mielec, aged 14
The eve of the Jewish New Year, people started preparing for the holiday, and of course it was busy everywhere … and the same day in the afternoon the Nazis marched in with tanks and motorbikes, and the roar was absolutely frightening.

Janina Dawidowicz, fleeing Warsaw with her family
The German army was marching in as we were coming out and I was very anxious to see the Germans. I was very curious and I wanted to see what they looked like. There were those enormous, unending streams of columns marching in as we were driving out all along the roads of course. The entire army was marching.

Roman Halter, Chodecz, aged 12

Well, when the *Wehrmacht* [German army] came through, that was quite all right and they kept saying. 'We are all right, we are fighters. We are *Wehrmacht*. But watch out. The people who are going to follow us, they are going to be quite different from us.' We didn't know what they meant.

> The main German army was known as the *Wehrmacht*. It pledged allegiance to Hitler, but had its own military traditions and was not wholly a 'Nazi army'. However, Hitler had created a separate organization known as the 'SS' (from the German word *Schutzstaffel*, meaning 'protection squad'), which was led by a fanatical Nazi called Heinrich Himmler. The SS were trained intensively as Nazi soldiers, and they became notorious for their brutal behaviour and absolute devotion to Hitler's ideas. It was the SS who ran Hitler's system of concentration camps. In Poland and Russia, Hitler ordered SS 'Action Groups' to follow the main German army. Their job was to round up Jews and force them into ghettos. They also acted as mobile execution squads.

From house to house

When the Nazis invaded countries in western Europe such as Holland and France they treated the general population with a degree of respect (though of course this did not extend to Jews). Thanks to Hitler's idea that the Slavs were 'inferior', this wasn't the case in Poland, where Nazi troops were encouraged to act brutally towards the population as a whole. Hitler had invaded Poland to get 'living space' for Germans, so the Nazis soon began forcing many Poles from their homes and shunting them further east, making way for settlers from Germany. But if Slavs were a lower race of humans in Hitler's eyes, then Slavic Jews were hardly human at all, and the Nazis – especially the SS – treated them accordingly.

Roman Halter

People were being humiliated right from the beginning. And that was considered a tremendous joke, getting hold of a Jewish person, making him scrub the pavement with some toothbrush or little brush, cutting off his beard. I then used to be the hairdresser for my father and grandfather because it was too dangerous to move out of the house with a beard. That was considered an invitation to be cut and molested and humiliated.

> For many eastern European Jewish men it was customary to wear a beard for religious reasons. By cutting off their beards, the Nazis were not only abusing them physically but also insulting their religion. The Nazis also set fire to many synagogues and banned Jews from worshipping in them.

Barbara Stimler

One day they came and took all the Jewish books, our praying books, and we had to carry them to the middle of the market place and burn them. They took also the rabbi [religious leader] and a cart. They took a cart without a horse, and he had to load up stones on it, and pull it and push it. It was a terrible scene and we all got very frightened.

Tauba Biber

Then they were going around from house to house, rounding up all the men around the synagogue. With their arms up, they had to stand, while the synagogue … it was all burning. We happened to live opposite. Luckily enough our house was[n't] burnt – a miracle. We sat in the house, afraid to cough or sneeze in the dark, and just occasionally peep out from behind the curtains to see what has happened. It was burning all night.

So in fear every day, the evenings we sit in the dark. We were afraid to switch a light on in case the Germans will know that we are in.

Even to listen when it was quiet to their footsteps in the street – it was absolutely terrifying.

Decrees went up

Before the War, the Nazis had spent six years making life so unpleasant for Germany's half-million Jews that by 1939 most of them had left. Now, having invaded half of Poland, Hitler had another two million Jews under his control. What was he to do with them? This was what he called the 'Jewish Question'.

It would not be long before the Nazis came up with a 'solution', but for now they just forced Jews to live under severe restrictions that were brutally enforced.

Tauba Biber

So the Germans settled in. They confiscated most possessions. Every day there was a new rule. Gold, silver … all valuables had to be given up. And also then they make demands of money, and all the time we were threatened.

Kitty Felix

Things changed for us almost instantly. We had no means of supporting ourselves, all the banks had been seized by the Germans – or all accounts had been frozen. Very soon decrees went up in the city, urging people to register. This was sort of the very first inkling that some sort of clamp-down was in progress. And we had to register and of course once we did that they knew where everybody lived, where everybody was. You couldn't move from one part of the city to another, you had to re-register or you had to have like an exit-permit to go from one place to another.

Edyta Klein

Within a few weeks every [Jewish] male or female over the age of 12 had to wear an armband with the Star of David. It had to be a certain width, and always clean, and sort of prominently displayed on the right arm, so they had no difficulties of recognizing the Jew on the street when they wanted one. This gave me freedom because I wasn't 12 years old so I could still go out on the street.

> The six-pointed Star of David, made up of two interlocking equilateral triangles, is an important Jewish symbol. The Nazis chose it as an easily recognizable sign that could be used to identify Jews. Today the Star of David appears on the national flag of Israel, the Jewish state that was founded in Palestine after the War.

Rena Litwak, Warsaw, aged 15

Life was very difficult and then they said we had to put on armbands. It was about five inches wide with the Star of David on it. If you didn't wear the armband they would shoot you.

Barbara Stimler

We had to have yellow stars. We were not allowed to walk on the pavement, but we had to walk in the middle of the road. You felt like an animal – very, very degrading.

Kitty Felix

I think there were armbands at one point. I didn't resent it at the time, I didn't really think anything of it. In fact, nothing disturbed me until a certain event, and that was when I walked the street with a friend, a boy of my age, and the decree was that when a patrol or German soldiers walked on the pavements, everybody else had to get off into the road. I stepped into the road, but my friend didn't and this patrol in uniform, the soldier, pulled out a gun and shot my friend in the head. And I'm afraid this was the very first time I realized the seriousness of the situation.

A young Jewish man in Warsaw, wearing the 'Star of David' armband

Janina Dawidowicz, Kalisz

We were thrown out of our house because German families were moving into the town and houses were needed for them. One by one all the members of the family were thrown out of their houses, and everything was confiscated. The occupants were told they must not take anything with them. Everything must be left as it is.

A lot of people were arrested. Some were killed; those who refused to leave were just shot in their houses. And we were stunned and helpless.

Janina Dawidowicz
The only change we could hope for was the end of the War. But the Germans were winning everything. Paris fell, France fell very quickly and the situation was getting worse every day. All the news was bad. The Germans seemed unstoppable.

Edyta Klein
My stepfather was caught on the street. He was wearing a beret and he didn't take off the beret fast enough in front of the Germans, and they beat him up. They broke his nose and so on, because every male had to take off a hat in front of a German.

Roman Halter
We suddenly realized that today was bad, but tomorrow will be even worse. And we wondered what would come.

Kitty Felix
The decrees went up very shortly after to announce that all Jews would have to move to a different part of the city. And what we didn't realize, of course, was that this was the very start of the [closed] ghettos.

The gates were closed

In order to make the rest of Poland 'Jew-free', the Nazis had decided to herd all Jews into the Jewish quarters that already existed in many Polish cities (including Warsaw, Lodz and Lublin). There they would be 'concentrated' together and isolated from the rest of Polish society while the Nazis decided what to do with them. As Jews from towns and villages all over Poland were crammed inside, the ghettos soon became dreadfully overcrowded. Many families had only a single room between them, and some didn't even have that.

Janina Dawidowicz, Warsaw

We went from one house to another and couldn't find anywhere where we could stay. Nobody had room. Warsaw was partly destroyed. We spent several hours just driving in a cab from one address to another and we ended up homeless in a part of Warsaw we didn't know at all. It was in fact the Warsaw Ghetto, though at that time there were no walls. It was the very poor part of Warsaw, where most of the poor Jewish population lived before the War.

We were simply sitting in that cab wondering what to do next. And the man living in the house just where we were, standing on the first floor, put his head out of the window and asked what we were doing. And then he came down, talked to us, and said they would take us in. He and his wife and a baby and the wife's parents were living in a little two-room flat, no bathroom, in a very, very poor little house. We were homeless and they took us in.

Then, when the ghettos were crammed with people, the Nazis turned them into gigantic prisons by forcing the Jews themselves to build walls and fences around them.

Janina Dawidowicz

We just found ourselves in the street which was incorporated into the ghetto and the ghetto was actually formed with the walls around it. At first nobody knew what the walls were for but eventually we found out, the gates were closed and we were all shut in.

A bridge over an Aryan street connecting two parts of the Warsaw Ghetto

In the Middle Ages, when anti-Semitism was widespread throughout Europe, many cities confined their Jewish population to ghettos, sometimes with walls around them. Unlike the Nazis' ghettos, however, the gates of medieval ghettos were usually only locked at night. In later centuries, walled ghettos were abolished – until the Nazis recreated them. The Warsaw Ghetto, the largest, was sealed off in November 1940. More than 350,000 people were crammed into an area of 1.3 square miles, with an average of seven people living in every room. The walls were 10 feet high and Jews caught trying to escape were shot.

Edyta Klein, Warsaw Ghetto

We were four people by that time and we were fortunate enough to have some friends to secure a room, in what was once a lovely flat. And it was overlooking the [wall]. The wall was built right in the middle of the road – so one side was ghetto side, the other side was a beautiful park. And we had what was a living room in this flat. And so I could look out

111

through the window and see children playing – sort of well fed, and sort of carefree. And here we were closed in the ghetto. We stayed in that room for 20 months. It was our living room, our bedroom, our loo.

Kitty Felix, Lublin Ghetto
Soon after the ghettos were formed there were horrendous incidents where people were just seized in the street, their heads were shaved, the men were dragged to shovel snow, they were beaten up. I've been seized to work, to scrub floors, very often beaten up and had to run back home in tears. But gradually we learned how to hide, the people began to make hiding places in the houses, particularly men. It was incredibly dangerous for men to venture on to the streets.

Its own organization

The ghettos became completely separate societies, cut off from the surrounding streets where the non-Jewish Poles lived. The Nazis forced the Jews in the ghettos to form their own governing councils and police forces, which meant that the Nazis themselves only rarely set foot inside the walls. The Jewish councils allocated housing, collected taxes (which often had to be handed over to the Germans), organized work parties, and ran hospitals and prisons – but they were completely dependent on the Nazis for their meagre food supply. Many ordinary Jews came to resent the Jewish councils and policemen for co-operating with the Nazis and doing their work for them.

Szmulek Gontarz, aged 10 in 1940 at formation of Lodz Ghetto
It is like a town, it had to have its own organization, it had to have its own police; it had to have its own officials and officers and so on. They organized factories where we worked, even though the products

went to the Germans. All this took some organization and there was a Jewish Committee who prepared all this. At the beginning they were very sympathetic to the people, but people change. These people, although they were Jewish, the sympathy had gone. The Germans were outside, we didn't see the Germans anymore. We just saw our own Jewish people mistreating us.

The ghetto in Lodz, Poland's second-largest city, was sealed off in May 1940. It was surrounded by barbed-wire fences, not walls, and guarded by SS units. There were more than 160,000 Jews inside – an average of about three or four people per room.

Janina Dawidowicz

When [the Nazis] did come to the ghetto it was to destroy, to kill, to arrest people. They used to go into shops and simply destroy them. They used to go into people's houses and destroy whatever they found, kill, murder, or just arrest people and take them off, and you never saw them again.

Kitty Felix

There was no means of communication with other ghettos and we didn't know what went on in other ghettos. It was much too dangerous to even contemplate listening to radios. Radios had to be given up at the very start, all radios had to be handed in. And of course searches were undertaken daily.

Janina Dawidowicz

My father found a job as a policeman, a Jewish policeman. Being a Jewish policeman was extremely unpopular and the family was horrified when he came home and told us. But it was the only job he could get. We were hoping at that time that there were policemen and policemen and he would be one of the good ones. He was a good man and he certainly would not be unjust or cruel, and he would do his duty. We didn't know then what eventually the duty of a Jewish policeman would be, that was just the beginning.

Shmuel Dresner, aged 12 at formation of Warsaw Ghetto

Nobody had enough food. People kept on selling things because bread became terribly expensive. You sold all your possessions gradually. We sold whatever we had, because there was no income coming in. There was a small percentage of people who were all right, that was the smugglers, underworld people who had contacts and also the people who were on top, like the Jewish police and people who were in the [Jewish Council]. The majority of people were just gradually selling everything off for some food.

A street market in the Warsaw Ghetto

Despite the dreadful circumstances inside the ghettos, people went to great lengths to show that they were not going to give up on normal life altogether.

Janina Dawidowicz

Schools were forbidden but the parents organized small groups of children, four or five at a time, and of course there was no lack of teachers. And we met once or twice a week in somebody's room – usually in a different room every week, because there was the death penalty for the children, the teachers, parents, in fact everybody in the house if they were discovered. And we had classes in just the basics. There were not enough books and the books were out of date. They were pre-[First World] War. But we learnt with great enthusiasm. There were university professors who were also giving courses in everything.

There were very good theatres in the Warsaw Ghetto, after all there were so many extremely good actors, actresses, singers, musicians. There were concerts, theatre performances, everything. There were clandestine libraries. I belonged to one of course because I read day and night.

My mother was extremely frightened, unhappy, bitter. But her reaction was to try and ignore what was going on and try and continue life as nearly normal as possible. That is why I had to have lessons and she was careful about children who I was allowed to play with, and I had strict rules about going out and coming home. In fact they were just trying to preserve the standards, in spite of the fact that we were living in this ghastly little room and that my parents were simply starving. Even with my father being a policeman we did not have enough to eat. My father was far too honest ever to abuse his powers.

■ ■ ■ ■ ■

People used to fight for a potato

As the months passed, the struggle against hunger became more and more desperate. The Nazis only allowed a tiny amount of food through the gates, and most people only received a fraction of what they needed to live on. Disease also spread rapidly in the overcrowded conditions.

Shmuel Dresner

People started dying from hunger. You saw them dying on the street. Children with swollen feet lying with their little sisters, begging for food. The trouble was that there was nobody who would give them anything, nobody had enough food.

Children living in Warsaw Ghetto

Edyta Klein

I remember being continuously hungry. And of course people didn't have the ingredients. I always had nightmares that probably a dog or a cat was in that pot.

Janina Dawidowicz

I think a 14- or 15-year-old body really needs food and you're quite ruthless then and this becomes an obsession. All you want is to eat and all your intelligence is: 'Where can I get something that is vaguely edible.'

Issy Rondell, aged 5 at formation of Warsaw Ghetto

If you didn't have any money you existed on what you could scratch out for yourself, by selling things or wheeling and dealing. People used to fight for a potato. I remember one occasion a wagon went by and a sack broke and potatoes went rolling out on to the street and hordes of people jumped on them.

Janina Dawidowicz

People used to eat things which are completely inedible. People ate potato peels. They were just chewing bits of wood. Small children, the toddlers, used to chew candle droppings, drips from the candle. People just ate whatever they found on the street, on the pavement.

Edyta Klein

Typhoid was rampant. It decimated the ghetto population. There was typhoid in every building. The only good part of this epidemic was that the Germans were afraid to venture deep into the ghetto. But the decimated population was replaced by the people from the outside, from the *shtetls* [villages], from the small towns. They were bringing them all in open vans or open horse carts, into the ghetto, and those people were in such horrible conditions, I can't even describe it.

The only way to get extra food was to smuggle it in from outside. This was an extremely dangerous job, since any one caught was liable to be shot. Even so, it was a job that was often done by children, who were small enough to squeeze through tiny holes in the walls and less likely to be challenged if spotted outside the ghettos.

Kitty Felix

There was very little contact with the outside population. The only contact was bartering and selling goods for food. It was up to the children and youngsters like me to obtain food. We very often went down the sewers and over to the [other] side, but this wasn't really possible for the adults, and especially too dangerous for men. My father realized that I had grown up overnight and I was pretty well the breadwinner in the family, because he couldn't get out and I couldn't go to school because children were not allowed to go to school in Lublin. In Lublin all school books were smashed up.

Issy Rondell

There was a high wall where the Germans used to patrol, but the place we used to go through was through some houses and cellars. I squeezed through a sewer and over a wall and into a cemetery. From the cemetery we used to make our way into Warsaw proper, through a park.

Albin Ossowski, Warsaw

Often children, out of hunger, escaped through little holes and went hiding on stairs in big houses. But people were afraid to take them in. Sometimes the families took them, washed them, fed them, but were afraid to keep them because if the Germans found out they were hiding some Jewish people, the punishment was they were shot.

■ ■ ■ ■ ■

Children would sometimes slip through holes in the ghetto walls
to try to get food from the outside

Some people in the streets outside the ghettos did risk their lives to help Jews, either by giving them food or by hiding them in their houses. (In Warsaw, several thousand Jews lived in hiding outside the ghetto walls.) But there were others who betrayed them.

Kitty Felix

Unfortunately it was the Poles who would identify the Jews for the Germans. So when I foraged for food on the [other] side and bartered clothes or any goods that my father would give me, it was the Poles who would say, 'Ah, here is a Jew. Oh, quickly, there's a patrol. We better just hand her in.' And very often I was handed over to a patrol, beaten up and thrown back into the ghetto without having brought anything back.

119

As the first year in the ghettos passed, life settled down into a kind of awful routine. People died every day, but most found ways to eke out some sort of existence. As they focused on the daily struggle to survive in the ghettos, none had any idea that the Nazis were already planning to send them somewhere even worse.

Kitty Felix

The time in the ghetto was a time of incredible fear, but gradually you became accustomed to fear and I think you took chances. But you lived with fear constantly.

Edyta Klein

[My family sat] every evening at the table in our little room and tried to think about it, and figure out how we will survive. But the thing was that everybody believed [that] somehow the War would be over. And if one just kept oneself clean, if one could just manage to get another crumb of bread, if one can just, you know, have another soup, whatever the soup was made from… So there was always hope.

■ ■ ■ ■ ■

Britain May–June 1940

10 May 1940 Following the resignation of Neville Chamberlain, Winston Churchill becomes Prime Minister. Some people accuse Chamberlain of not doing enough in the war against Hitler.

14 May 1940 As German troops encircle the British army near Dunkirk, the Government sets up the Local Defence Volunteers (later known as the Home Guard) to defend Britain against possible invasion. They are a poorly equipped 'army' of volunteers aged between 17 and 65.

May 1940 Amid growing fear of invasion, thousands of German refugees in Britain are interned (imprisoned) as 'enemy aliens'.

27 May–4 June 1940 A huge fleet of Royal Navy ships, ordinary passenger ships and smaller boats (some of them crewed by their fishermen owners) rescue most of the British army from the beaches of Dunkirk, which are under heavy attack from the Germans.

10 June 1940 Italy joins the War on Germany's side, and a few days' later attacks France from the south. Germany and Italy – known as the Axis powers – will be joined by Japan later in the year.

22 June 1940 France surrenders to Germany, leaving only Britain (along with her overseas Empire) to fight the Axis powers. Everyone expects Germany to invade Britain next and thousands of British families register their children for a new scheme to evacuate them overseas to countries such as Australia, Canada and the United States.

21–24 June 1940 The Channel Islands, British territory off the French coast in the English Channel, are under imminent threat of invasion. Thirty thousand people are evacuated from the Islands to mainland Britain.

28–30 June 1940 The Channel Islands are attacked from the air and invaded by German troops.

Twenty-one miles

Britain: May–June 1940

All fleeing the same foe 124
That was the Home Guard 129
He looks like a spy 131
The doorbell rang 133
Halfway through *The Wizard of Oz* 136

All fleeing the same foe

If the first few months of the War had been surprisingly quiet in Britain, all that certainly changed in the early summer of 1940, when the country suddenly found itself on the brink of defeat. By then, many evacuees had returned to their homes, their families not realizing what lay in store. But as the British army was being rescued from the beaches of Dunkirk, and much of western Europe came within Hitler's grasp, a German invasion of Britain seemed increasingly likely.

British troops returning from France after Dunkirk

Joanna Rogers, returned from evacuation to her home in Croydon in 1940

There was more evidence of war at home than there was in Brighton. Signposts had all been taken down. We had the fire station near us, we had the siren. We found a lot of things sandbagged. Daddy had improved the [bomb] shelter; he was growing melons on the top, melons and marrows. The 'Dig for Victory' thing was going and everyone was growing.

After 30 May 1940, signposts and street names were removed throughout the country so that the Germans would not be able to find their way around if they invaded. And in preparation for bombing, buildings had been sandbagged to protect people from blast damage. Meanwhile, 'Dig for Victory' was a campaign to persuade people to grow their own food, either in their gardens or in allotments.

Joanna Rogers

Our new school started off the morning with 'Land of Hope and Glory' and we were intensely patriotic. In our dining room we had a *Daily Telegraph* war map and we had little flags. Every day we would listen to the radio and we would move the flags, and they were steadily going backwards across France – backwards and backwards. And we were getting a little bit apprehensive. I remember my parents getting more and more depressed about it, but we just went on going to school as usual.

We did at that time begin to start going to the cinema. We used to go Saturday mornings to a children's show. They used to have newsreel – Pathé and Gaumont – and that was the first time we ever saw moving pictures of war, and I think we began to take it a little more seriously then.

Newsreels lasted about ten minutes and were shown before the main film at cinemas. Pathé and Gaumont were two of the most well-known companies who produced them.

As British families absorbed the news coming from across the Channel, they realized that it could be only a matter of time before the Germans launched a full-scale attack on Britain. This caused a fresh wave of evacuation from the south-east coast, the most vulnerable area.

A barrage balloon in a London park

■ ■ ■ ■ ■

Sylvia Parkes, evacuated from Margate, Kent, to Staffordshire in 1940, aged 13

We were being evacuated from a suspected invasion on our coast. They could quite easily have landed over here. We were only 21 miles away from where they were. So I suppose they thought they'd get us out of it before the necessity arose. The day we left, the boats [bringing troops back from Dunkirk] were coming in to Margate, not that we could see very clearly, it was only just a sort of blur of activity at the end of the pier.

I can remember going through London, presumably on the outskirts. But I remember there we saw the first barrage balloons. And I was thrilled to bits with them, I thought they were wonderful. And I remember saying to [my brother], 'You know, they look like great grey elephants.' And [he] wasn't a bit interested. He was wanting his mum by then and he couldn't have cared less.

Barrage balloons were filled with hydrogen gas and floated on long steel cables. They were designed to act as obstacles to low-flying dive-bombers (German planes which dived down and dropped their bombs right over their target).

When we got a little further along the line somewhere we stopped at a station where we had a whole lot of Belgian soldiers on the platform. And they were giving them orange drinks and things. And they shared them with the children. Fruit they'd been given, they shared with the children on the train. And there we were, grown men from a foreign country and little mites from the south-east. And we were all together, all fleeing from the same foe.

The soldiers who had been brought back from France were mostly British, but also included French and Belgians. They were a bedraggled, defeated army, but thankful to have escaped capture. Some had been brought back on fishing boats crewed by volunteer fishermen from the south-east coast.

Margaret Butler, re-evacuated from Portsmouth to Winchester in 1940, aged 12

A couple of the girls that I knew lost their fathers [at Dunkirk]. One of them was killed in the Navy. And another girl, her father had one of these small boats that went in to bring the troops home. And his little boat was sunk. And I can remember walking home with this girl and she was telling me about it. I think she just accepted it. Having lived apart from your family for that time you couldn't take it in that it had really happened. It was sort of something unreal.

Derek Milton, from Kennington, south London, aged 10

Things looked very, very gloomy – but nobody got disheartened about it. Churchill made a speech: 'We'll fight on the beaches, we'll fight in the streets…' and so forth. And I think everybody kind of rallied round the man. He was the right man at the right time.

Prime Minister Winston Churchill on a visit to Manchester in 1941

Winston Churchill became Prime Minister of Britain just a few hours after Hitler launched his attack in the west. Churchill was a popular leader who had warned of the dangers of Hitler for many years. He made his most famous speech on 4 June 1940, just after Dunkirk:

'We shall go on to the end ... we shall fight on the seas and oceans, we shall fight ... in the air, we shall fight on the beaches, we shall fight on the landing grounds, we shall fight in the fields and in the streets, we shall fight in the hills; we shall never surrender.'

Not everybody was so confident, and some families decided to send their children out of the country altogether. When the Government set up a special scheme to help poorer families send their children to North America it received over 200,000 applications.

Alan Maynard, evacuated from London to Essex and then to Montreal, Canada, aged 13
I didn't like being evacuated. I was always running home. Until finally my parents said, 'Oh well, there's nothing much happening in London.' So my parents allowed me to come home. Then of course Dunkirk came and that was when they decided that I ought to go to Canada. They didn't think their chances were very good and they wanted me to be safe and out of the way. And Canada and America seemed very safe.

That was the Home Guard

As a last-ditch defence against invasion, in May 1940 the Government had set up the 'Local Defence Volunteers', later renamed the 'Home Guard'. Made up of more than a million volunteers between the ages of 17 and 65, the Home Guard had limited training and was very poorly equipped. Nevertheless, it gave people the feeling that they were doing something useful at a time of crisis. Boys under 17 were sometimes allowed to join.

Home Guard members on military exercises

Charles Carrington, Derby Home Guard, aged 16

We had an exercise where the regular army were going to theoretically attack Derby and the Home Guard was going to defend. Well, my number two and myself went into our little bunker. While we were there the brigadier of the regular forces approached along the railway track and he was about 5 yards off us before he realized that there was a gun poking through. And he congratulated us on the camouflage. 'But you've forgotten one thing. You've forgotten your line of retreat.'

To which my reply was, 'Well, if they've got this far, Brigadier, we haven't got any retreat. We're dead. So we didn't bother with it.'

Stan Poole, north London Home Guard, aged 14

One time, in came this major, and he's got a 4-foot length of scaffold tubing with an 18-inch bayonet welded into it. This was one of these 'pikes'. And I was always keen on arms, and I'd got books on arms, everything. And he came in with this and he was saying what a wonderful weapon [it was].

And I said to him, in all my innocence, 'Excuse me, sir. What use would these be against a German *Schmeisser* MP40 [sub-machine gun]?'

That was the Home Guard.

He looks like a spy

During that summer, no one knew when or where the Germans might arrive in Britain. Would they land on the beaches of seaside towns? Or would they land by parachute, as they had done in Holland? (In June the ringing of church bells in Britain was banned, except to warn of a German invasion.) There was also a growing fear of enemy secret agents and spies who may already have landed in the country. As people went about their daily lives, they were told to keep an eye out for anything suspicious, especially people speaking with a German accent or not knowing their way around.

Eric Hill, Southampton, aged 8

We were very conscious not to talk to strangers in case they were Germans. We thought every stranger was a German spy. If you saw a stranger, you'd think, 'Oh, he looks like a German spy.' So you didn't talk about anything. You more or less kept out of his way.

The Government tried to persuade people not to say too much to strangers, or even gossip with their neighbours, in case they were overheard and accidentally gave away vital information.

CARELESS TALK COSTS LIVES

A Government poster showing Hitler eavesdropping on gossiping civilians

Walter Hayman, emigrated from Germany to Britain with his father in 1937, aged 14 in 1940

There was one occasion when my father was accused by one of the neighbours of being a German spy. It was a ludicrous suggestion but people were of course somewhat afraid. And I think perhaps he'd been using a torch and they said that he was signalling. It all blew over. But that kind of thing did happen from time to time.

From Germany the Nazis added to the panic by broadcastingradio announcements in English that spoke about a coming invasion. Their most famous broadcaster became known as 'Lord Haw-Haw' because of his plummy British accent. Rumours soon spread that Haw-Haw was in touch with a network of German undercover agents who were poised to take over the country.

The doorbell rang

The growing hysteria caused by the invasion threat eventually led to widespread fears that German refugees might be secret supporters of Hitler. As soon as war had begun, the British Government had worried that some Germans living in Britain might pose a threat to 'national security', and it had already labelled them all as 'enemy aliens'.

Inge Engelhard, German Jewish refugee, Coventry

Suddenly, instead of being a very interesting little refugee, I became a Nazi! I was so upset, because it was so unfair. But I also had friends and my friends were very nice.

Dorothy Oppenheimer, German Jewish refugee, Leeds

It's really the name that was more upsetting than anything. And my fellow pupils just laughed me out of it and said, 'Don't worry, we know you're not an enemy alien!'

However, the invasion scare of 1940 led to more severe measures. After a newspaper campaign had turned the tide of opinion against them, the Government eventually decided to arrest almost all 'aliens' over the age of 16. Most were sent to prison camps – known as 'internment camps' – on the Isle of Man (an island in the Irish Sea).

Dorothy Oppenheimer, aged 12 when her father was interned in May 1940

The [door]bell rang and they came and said, 'Mr Oppenheimer, I'm afraid you have to come with us.' And he was taken to the Isle of Man. To have escaped from the Nazis and then to be locked up and away from my mother, it must have been absolutely dreadful.

Barbara Isralowitz, aged 16 when she was interned

The police came one morning and they knocked at the door and they said, 'You are now going to be interned.' And I packed a suitcase, and I asked whether I could make a phone call and I phoned [a friend] and said, 'I am being interned.' And they took me and we went in a coach to Liverpool, and one sort of felt, 'Well, I wonder what will happen next.' We boarded a ship and somebody said to me, 'You seem very calm.' And I replied, 'Well, there's not much point in being anything else.'

After 10 June, when Italy entered the War, the 20,000 Italians living in Britain at the time also became 'enemy aliens' and 4,000 of them were immediately interned.

For the Germans and Italians sent to the Isle of Man, conditions were fairly relaxed and most prisoners managed to eke out a tolerable existence.

Henry Fulda, Jewish refugee from Munich, interned with his father on Isle of Man in 1940, aged 17

The perimeter was guarded but there were very few guards there. We were taken out for walks every day, perhaps 50 or 60 of [us], and there were three or four guards walking alongside us. We walked past shops and they didn't stop people from dashing in and buying some sweets and then falling back into line. It was very relaxed. My father referred to the place as a holiday camp, particularly as he had experienced Dachau concentration camp.

An internment camp at Douglas, on the Isle of Man

Even so, many internees resented their loss of freedom and the fact that they had been taken away from their families at a time of great danger. And not all internees were treated so well. Thousands of men and teenage boys were judged too 'dangerous' to stay in Britain and were deported to internment camps in Canada and Australia. They included many refugees from the Nazis as well as people who had lived happily in Britain for several years.

On 1 July 1940, a ship called the Arandora Star *set sail for Canada carrying 1,500 internees. On the way it was torpedoed by a German submarine and 650 drowned. The ship was only carrying lifeboats for 1,000 passengers. A few days later another ship, the* Dunera, *sailed to Australia with 2,500 internees aboard, including a number of survivors from the* Arandora Star. *Conditions were appalling, with outbreaks of dysentery in the cramped living quarters below decks, and the internees were badly treated by their guards. The voyage lasted seven weeks. These episodes caused a scandal in Britain and eventually led to the release of most internees before the end of the War. On release, many of them joined the armed services and helped to defeat Hitler.*

Halfway through The Wizard of Oz

If anyone needed reminding where the real danger lay, it came at the end of June when the Germans invaded the Channel Islands (the British islands of Jersey, Guernsey, Alderney and Sark in the English Channel). As soon as France fell to the Germans in June 1940 it seemed likely that the islands would be invaded, and Churchill decided they could not be defended without heavy loss of life. About a third of the population – including most of Guernsey's schoolchildren – managed to scramble away to the relative safety of Britain. Then, on 28 June, German planes swooped down and attacked a row of tomato lorries in St Peter Port, the capital of Guernsey. Expecting the islands to be heavily defended, the Germans had mistaken the lorries for troop carriers. Within two days, the islands were occupied.

Desmond McGarry, Georgetown, Jersey, aged 11

I remember one day going into our garden and seeing a large German plane sweeping very low over our house and I saw the markings, and we were in a state of apprehension because we didn't really know what was going on. And there were so many people trying to get out of the island, and I can remember a long queue stretching down to the boats and people were trying to escape on coal boats or any other vessel that might take them to England. Around about that time I attended a film at the Forum Cinema, and it was *The Wizard of Oz*, and it was about halfway through when there was this almighty explosion and the seat was shaken, and shortly after that the film stopped and the manager came on stage and said the islands were under attack by the Germans and that we'd have to take shelter. So I never saw the rest of it.

A British policeman talking to a German officer in Jersey after occupation

Stella Metcalfe, Jersey, aged 9

We were on the beach with my aunt. I remember the machine-gunning overhead. We made just one mad dash up to our landlady's house. The landlady put a blanket over the window in case of flying glass. We remained there for a couple of hours, then went home. We were invited by friends to join them in the cellar. But then leaflets were dropped which asked everyone to put out white flags. We hung something out the window, whether it was a pillowcase or not I can't remember. When we woke up the next day there were all these notices up everywhere and a few Germans beginning to walk about.

Desmond McGarry

My first sight [of German troops] was at the harbour. I remember feeling almost as though they came from another world. I couldn't get used to their jackboots and their grey-green uniform. And of course they were heavily armed. Though one of them gave my friend and myself a couple of bullets from his rifle. They didn't give the impression that they were going to do anything adverse. They wanted to show that they were so very proud to have occupied the only part of the British Empire that was then occupied, and they wanted to put on a good show. I as a boy was very impressed by their marching. They were so well-built and well turned out and their singing was quite impressive.

> The Germans stayed on the Channel Islands for five years, turning them into a heavily defended fortress where thousands of troops were stationed. Islanders were forbidden to leave, or listen to radios, and children were forced to learn German at school. Several slave-labour camps for prisoners of war were set up, and in 1942 about 2,000 islanders were deported to internment camps in Germany. Conditions on the islands later became very difficult because of food shortages.

■ ■ ■ ■ ■

Britain July–September 1940

July 1940 In preparation for 'Operation Sea Lion' – the full-scale invasion of Britain – the German air force (or Luftwaffe) begins to carry out raids against shipping in the English Channel and against military targets in the south-east of England. Meanwhile Hitler assembles an invasion fleet to bring his armies across the Channel.

1 August 1940 The SS Volendam, a ship packed with evacuees heading for Canada, is torpedoed by a U-boat in the Atlantic Ocean. The ship stays afloat and is towed back to Liverpool with no loss of life.

13 August 1940 Air supremacy is vital to Hitler's plans so he orders the Luftwaffe to attack Britain's airfields, hoping to destroy Britain's air-defence system. The Royal Air Force's Fighter Command struggles to cope with the onslaught. This is the beginning of what Winston Churchill describes as the 'Battle of Britain'.

August–September 1940 Air battles rage over Britain every day, especially in the south-east, as the Spitfires and Hurricanes of RAF Fighter Command try to shoot down German planes before they bomb RAF airfields. Although the Germans suffer greater losses than the British, the RAF – which is much smaller than the Luftwaffe – soon becomes desperately short of planes and pilots, bringing it very close to breaking point.

15 August 1940 The Luftwaffe launches its biggest attack so far, flying up to 2,000 sorties over Britain. Seventy-five German planes are shot down or crash, but a few reach the outskirts of London for the first time, bombing Croydon airport and the surrounding area.

20 August 1940 In a famous speech, Prime Minister Winston Churchill praises the RAF pilots defending Britain: 'Never in the field of human conflict was so much owed by so many to so few.' About 2,900 RAF pilots take part in the battle. Around one in six of them are from countries other than Britain – mainly Poland, Czechoslovakia and Canada.

24 August 1940 German planes drift off course and accidentally bomb central London. Churchill believes it is a deliberate attack on civilians and orders reprisal raids on Berlin, the German capital, which take place a few days later, killing several civilians.

4 September 1940 Hitler makes a speech promising revenge: 'In England they're filled with curiosity and keep asking, "Why doesn't he come?"... Be calm, be calm. He's coming! He's coming! ... We will raze their cities to the ground!' The Luftwaffe is ordered to prepare for full-scale attacks on British cities. However, by switching the main attack away from Britain's airfields, Germany will give the RAF a much-needed opportunity to rebuild its strength.

17 September 1940 On its way to Canada, an evacuation ship, the SS City of Benares, is torpedoed by a German U-boat. Over 250 people lose their lives including 77 evacuee children. Two weeks later the Government suspends its overseas evacuation scheme.

On the seas and in the air

Britain: July–September 1940

'Where are ours?' 142

'They'll get to London one day soon' 145

Cowboys and Indians in the sky 146

'What a waste of ice cream!' 149

'Where are ours?'

During the Battle of Britain much of the fighting took place high up in the skies above cloud level, or out over the English Channel. But on a clear day vapour trails (or 'con' trails) could often be seen across the skies. For some children – especially those who lived along the south-east coast or in the Home Counties – there was always a chance of seeing a dogfight between British and German fighters, or a pilot bailing out in a parachute, or even coming across a crashed German plane.

Pauline de Guerrin, Herne Bay, Kent coast, aged 18

It was tremendous. I used to see waves of bombers coming over and we used to jump up and down and say, 'Where are ours? Where are ours?' And then out of the blue would come just a few fighter planes and break up these formations and we'd scream and cheer as though we were at a football match.

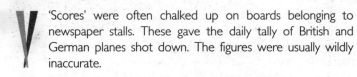

'Scores' were often chalked up on boards belonging to newspaper stalls. These gave the daily tally of British and German planes shot down. The figures were usually wildly inaccurate.

Pauline de Guerrin

We did see some awful things as well. I mean, I saw pilots being brought in in boats and you couldn't tell which one was an Englishman and which one was a German. They were just young men looking grey in the face with exhaustion, and miserable and wet. They just looked like young men who'd had a rotten time. They'd had a fight, over the bay, and they'd shot each other down.

As more and more RAF planes were lost, people in Britain were encouraged to collect scrap metal for recycling into replacements. Children often helped to collect old pots and pans and other unwanted items. Sometimes they helped to raise money for a local 'Spitfire Fund', where individual towns paid for a new aeroplane. There was even a 'price list' of parts, and although a wing would cost £2,000, a rivet was only sixpence, so every bit of pocket money helped.

Soldiers collecting for a 'Spitfire Fund' sitting on the fuselage of a crashed German Heinkel bomber

Joanna Rogers, returned evacuee, Croydon, east London, aged 10

We had joined the Girl Guides and we had begun to collect things. We used to collect salvage and we used to collect paper. And at the time they were beginning to collect metal and we gave the railings of our house – they weren't railings, they were chain, thick chain links. Sometime during that summer they went. First of all you gave them, I think in the end they were asked for, but I think my father was very proud of us giving ours first in our road. And I think they asked for saucepans for Spitfires but I don't think my mother parted with any. But as Girl Guides we did go round collecting.

More serious for the RAF than the shortage of aeroplanes was the shortage of pilots. In August 1940 it was losing almost ten per cent of its pilots every week, and there was very little time to train replacements.

The inside of an Anderson shelter

'They'll get to London one day soon'

As the summer wore on, the Luftwaffe's raids on air-defences in the south-east of Britain increased, and many people expected that bombs would soon be falling on Britain's cities. By this time more than two million households had been issued with an 'Anderson' bomb shelter (named after the Home Secretary). Made out of corrugated iron, it was designed to be placed in a hole dug in the garden, with earth packed on top. Although they were cold, damp and uncomfortable, they protected anyone inside from everything except a direct hit. Air-raid sirens had also been set up in built-up areas, to warn people of incoming aircraft.

Joanna Rogers

There were odd raids in Kent and Sussex and Surrey, and we used to say, 'Oh, you know, they'll get to London one day soon.'

Then I remember very clearly a summer day the sirens went seriously the first time for us. It was sunny and it was the middle of the day and we immediately repaired to the shelter, which was the first time we'd seriously gone down there. Now Daddy had built it and he'd put bunks in it for the four of us. The bottom two bunks my parents were going to have and the top two bunks we were going to have. And he'd made the framework out of wood with chicken wire in between and mattresses and Elizabeth and I used to laugh because the chicken wire sagged horribly and it would be very difficult for people sleeping under it – we would have been given the upper bunks.

But I remember very clearly this day going to the shelter. Mother, Elizabeth and I sat in it and father stood just outside. And he said, 'Look! Quick, here's a *Junkers!*'

I remember it clearly to this day and it flew fairly low over us and hit Croydon Airport. And that was the first raid on London.

I don't think we were frightened. We were excited. I mean Daddy was the sort of person who would say, 'Quick, come and look', whereas mother would say, 'No, stay in.' But Daddy had us out and we saw the *Junkers* and we saw the bombs dropped. And we were thrilled, Elizabeth and I – something was happening, you know. We saw the bombs come out of it, he was fairly low. Mind you, as Daddy pointed out, they weren't falling on us.

Cowboys and Indians in the sky

By late August, German raiders were coming over more and more frequently, sometimes passing over London on their way to or from targets in other parts of the country. Bombs began to fall along the south coast, in Wales, on Merseyside, and in the Midlands. But this was still only a foretaste of what was to come.

Sylvia Limburg, from Marylebone, central London
I remember seeing aeroplanes chasing each other in the searchlights. I remember standing on the corner where we lived and watching the searchlights playing in the sky, seeing aeroplanes chasing each other like little silver crosses in the searchlights. It was like watching cowboys and Indians in the sky.

Joanna Rogers
Elizabeth and I used our bicycles a great deal and we used to cycle to Keston, which is about six miles from us, and there was a very big 15-inch gun installed there, which we called 'Keston Kate'. And we were extremely interested. It was very sandbagged in, but we could see

the barrel and it looked enormous to us. We weren't often there when it went off but the whole ground shook round about and you could see dust rising off the ground. But of course we weren't allowed to get terribly near it.

Children watching from a trench as planes fight in the skies above the south-east of England

Derek Milton, from Kennington, south London, aged 10

You got the planes coming over and you could look up at the sky and you could see the con trails in the sky where the battles were going on.

Half the street used to stand out watching it – stupidly, because there were anti-aircraft guns firing and shrapnel coming all over the place. And like an idiot I'd stand out there star-gazing at it.

Anti-aircraft guns and searchlights were stationed along the coast and around many cities. The guns were hopelessly inaccurate, and hardly ever brought down any enemy planes. They also hurled jagged bits of metal casing far and wide, and it was often said that they did more harm to civilians as a result of falling shrapnel than to enemy aircraft. Nevertheless, they did force German bombers to fly higher, which meant that they couldn't drop bombs so accurately.

Joanna Rogers

We were finding shrapnel, and as the fire station was near to us this shrapnel on the road caused a lot of punctures. And we were given money for every bucketful of shrapnel we could take back to the fire station, and we used to scour the roads for it everywhere.

Dennis Hayden, evacuee in Newbury

One [plane] crashed very close to the school and we all cheered and said, 'Hooray that's the school!' We went next morning hoping to see it smashed to the ground. But there was the school, still standing. But the other side of the village this German plane had crashed in the field, and we all climbed over it and took goodness knows what off this thing, and took them all to school. Then about 11 o'clock the police turned up and soldiers, and said, 'No doubt you children have seen the plane that's crashed. Can we have anything you've taken?' And everyone was lifting up desk lids and handing back machine guns and pistols and belts of ammunition.

■ ■ ■ ■ ■

'What a waste of ice cream!'

While all this was going on, children were still being sent to Canada as part of the Government's evacuation scheme. Everyone knew that German submarines – known as 'U-boats'– were prowling the Atlantic and sinking ships carrying essential supplies to Britain. But the Government assured parents that the crossing was relatively safe, reminding them that ships would sail in large groups called convoys, escorted by armed Royal Navy ships that could help to defend them against attack.

When 406 people boarded the SS City of Benares *in September 1940, these assurances were no doubt firmly in their minds. In peacetime the 11,000-ton liner had been used to ply back and forth between Britain and India, and now she was to be the biggest in a convoy of 20 ships heading from Liverpool to Canada. Among the passengers were 90 evacuee children – some travelling privately but the majority as part of the Government's new scheme.*

Derek Bech, private evacuee with his mother and two sisters, aged 9

We were told to go down to the docks and we saw this lovely gleaming golden-grey ship, two funnels and this sort of peach colour underneath. It was a lovely sight. So we made ourselves at home and looked around the ship. We found our table at dinner and we were so impressed. We had a menu of so many choices, unbelievable because we had had rationing. And we went on this voyage, a very pleasant voyage. We ate and did everything we wanted. We explored the ship and made our own friends.

Ken Sparks, evacuee from the Government scheme, aged 13

Each day we had lessons, and we were being taught about the Canadian way of life and how they managed and what to expect. And we could play games and talk and such forth. We were allowed on deck and it was lovely. All them ships and the destroyers going up and down. Oh it was nice. We didn't think anything would happen. It was much too big a convoy to have any problems.

However, escort ships were in short supply, and after four days, as the City of Benares *convoy reached the middle of a choppy Atlantic, its escort was ordered to peel away and join up with a convoy heading in the other direction. Few of those on board realized that the ship was now undefended. In any case, they'd been told that it was difficult for U-boats to attack in rough weather.*

Colin Ryder Richardson, private evacuee, travelling without his parents, aged 11

I was in bed, and I was just about to go to sleep. I'd put a ball bearing that I seemed to have acquired in the top drawer of my desk between the two bunks, just to see how rough the sea was, because it would click from one side to the other as it rolled backwards and forwards. And it was a comforting sound because if I could hear that clicking I thought, well, we were not going to be torpedoed.

Derek Bech

And then at ten o'clock at night we were all asleep and I can remember waking up and hearing not an explosion but a thud: *boooooom*.

My mother said 'Get up'. So I got dressed and put on my school trousers, and I put on my school blazer, my school raincoat and even my school cap. We must have looked as if we were going out for a nice little boat-ride!

So we went up the main stairwell to the lounge. There was no panic. And we just waited there. And people started to hear rumours that we might have hit another boat.

After ten minutes the door from the deck burst open. It was blowing a gale outside and the ship was pitching up and down. And [an officer] came in, he just said, 'The ship is sinking fast. Go straight to your boats.'

Passengers had been drilled for emergencies, so most people knew where to go. But the weather conditions made launching the lifeboats extremely difficult. As they swung about in gale-force winds, several of them tipped up and threw their occupants into the sea. Other lifeboats became wedged against the side of the tilting ship.

Colin Ryder Richardson, escaped in a waterlogged lifeboat
We were told that as the ship was sinking it would suck everything down with it. And we were still bumping up against the hull. But somehow the waves managed to break us away from the liner and I suppose it was only about 30 yards when we saw the ship beginning to go down and the bows coming up and up and up. There was quite a lot of rush and noise, and then it slid down. I turned away for a moment and when I turned back it was gone.

Derek Bech, escaped on an emergency raft with his mother, sister and three other people
When we first were in the water we heard a lot of crying and screaming. And then of course the ship sank literally in front of our eyes. We were very close to it and it heeled right up in the air and then it fell slightly sideways on to where we were, and then it slid away from us. The ship still had all its lights on, it was a blaze of lights. And it went. And our first reaction, Sonia and I, we said: 'What a waste of ice cream!'

Because we'd lived with all this ice cream, as much as we could eat. And we said, 'Fancy all that going down.'

By now, all the other ships in the convoy had scattered. This was normal practice, to prevent them becoming sitting targets for a second torpedo attack, but it left the survivors of the City of Benares *to fend for themselves.*

Derek Bech

It was rough, it was cold – it was the North Atlantic in September – it was blowing a gale. We had hailstones. We went through squalls. There was a full moon, and the clouds would come rushing over and then all of a sudden it would go pitch dark and then we'd get these hailstones.

We were five people on the raft. It was wooden duckboarding and old kerosene drums, all held together with nails and rope. We were like a little cork going up and down. And we were hanging on with our fingers and every time these cylinders came up they pinched our fingers. And it was beginning to knock the nails out of the raft.

Sonia Bech

I had to use every ounce of energy and brain keeping myself on this bit of wood. It was up to me to hang on and I was a tough little thing, luckily. And I just fought for my life. But twice during the night I fell off. The first time I was absolutely sure that I'd drowned. I remember thinking, 'I wonder what God is going to be like.'

Derek Bech

My mother said, 'Sonia, swim like you've never swam in your life.' And this engineer pulled her onboard. And so we were sitting in our raft in the pitch dark and we were conscious of things bumping into us, flotsam and deck chairs and things like that. And you could see one or

152

two of the lifeboats had little lanterns on them, you could see the odd light flickering, but as the night went on they all disappeared.

Colin Ryder Richardson

Any movement just made people vulnerable. You had to sit as still as possible, holding on for dear life. We were trying to think of keeping our spirits up and although we sang a few songs, the storm soon put paid to this. And [we were] shouting to other people, 'Is there anybody out there?' Because if you're in the sea without a lifeboat the end is pretty quick. There was no way that any of us in the lifeboat could really help them, because if you stood up you were likely to be swept out.

Derek Bech

By daybreak we were very much on our own but we were on this sort of big dipper and when we were on the top of a wave you could see around you. And we did see fairly close by the mast of a small boat. And you could only see each other when you were both on top of a wave. If one's on top and the other down below you wouldn't see each other. So it was only every ten minutes or so that we could see each other. Anyway he came alongside and picked us up. He was the lifeboat from another ship that had been hit.

Eventually, on the afternoon following the night of the attack, Royal Navy ships arrived on the scene to search for survivors.

Colin Ryder Richardson, picked up on 18 September by the destroyer *HMS Hurricane*

So when we saw the destroyer it was almost beyond belief. And they had scrambling nets along the side of the ship, and asked us to climb up but it was impossible. I was [stiff] like a statue. So the sailors came down and we were hauled up and we were taken to the gallery of the engine room where we could dry out.

The destroyer was constantly stopping and starting, to pick up other survivors. But of course it all had to be done very quickly because there was no knowledge as to whether or not the sub was in the area and the destroyer itself would be vulnerable.

And the next day it was a lovely sunny day and it was very nice to be back on board a ship. And the sailors couldn't do enough for us, whatever we wanted we got if they could get it. A wireless operator gave me his badge as a memento.

Survivors from the *City of Benares* on the deck of *HMS Hurricane*, the ship that rescued them

Other survivors from the torpedoed ship drifted at sea for over a week before they were picked up.

Ken Sparks, survived in an open lifeboat for eight days with about 40 other people

We squashed together for warmth, it was awfully cold. And of course it was raining like mad and the wind was blowing a force-eight gale. And of course we had to bale the boat out. There was very little food. We had a ship's biscuit or a piece of peach or a piece of sardine per day, and a sip of water per day. And it kept us alive. Initially we were quite fit but after a couple of days with next to no food we got quite lethargic. I was rather lucky in that I'd still got my overcoat. Although it was sodden wet at least it kept some of the cold winds out.

Once, about three or four days out, we were surrounded by a pod of whales, but we had to chase them away because [they] could have smashed the boat to pieces. And then on the fifth day we saw a merchant ship, not very far away. We made a lot of noise and waved, but it didn't see us.

That was a big disappointment. The steward was the officer in charge. He decided which way we were going to go. [And] the morale kept up. Everybody thought we'd be picked up today or tomorrow or the day after. And if we weren't going to be picked up then we were going to row all the way to Ireland, we didn't care. I don't think anybody gave up hope.

Eventually 150 survivors from the City of Benares *were picked up, including 13 children. Within days of the tragedy, which became headline news all round the world, the Government cancelled its overseas evacuation scheme.*

Colin Ryder Richardson

By 20 September we were back in [Britain]. And we got into some assembly shed and were confronted by [people] asking for our passports and what had we to declare! Which was about the first thing that really made us laugh.

And all at once the newspaper reporters were on us and everything was so confusing. The next day my mother turned up. It seemed so incredible to see [her] again. It was like a sudden walking back in time after such an adventure. In the meantime my father had seen a picture of me on the front page of a newspaper on a railway platform and he went up to one of the passengers and said, 'That appears to be my son.' And that's how my father first knew about the whole event.

Sonia Bech, Colin Ryder Richardson and Derek Bech after their rescue

Britain and the Blitz 1940–1941

7 September 1940 The first mass air raid on London targets the East End dockyards. The 'Battle of Britain' is still going on, but this marks the beginning of what the British call the 'Blitz' (from the German word 'blitzkrieg': 'lightning war'). London will be heavily bombed every night until 14 November (except for 2 November when bad weather hampers the Luftwaffe).

11 September 1940 In a speech, Churchill compares the situation with the time when England faced invasion from the Spanish Armada. 'Every man and woman will therefore prepare himself to do his duty…'

15 September 1940 An enormous formation of German bombers is partly broken up by the RAF. Although many of the bombers do reach London, and cause terrible damage, the Germans suffer heavy losses and the morale of the RAF is lifted. Less than a fortnight later, another huge German attack is broken up over Kent. Only 30 out of 300 bombers get through to London.

30 September 1940 The last major air-battle in daylight marks the end of the 'Battle of Britain'. Hitler has called off the invasion of Britain, and instead makes plans to invade the Soviet Union. However, he orders the Luftwaffe to continue its attacks on British cities. Britain has survived the threat of invasion, but will have to endure another eight months of Blitz, with German bombers now coming mostly at night when the RAF can do little to stop them.

October–November 1940 Whilst continuing to bomb London, the Luftwaffe widens its attack to other towns and cities, including Birmingham, Coventry, Portsmouth, Southampton, Liverpool, Hull, Glasgow and Belfast. The worst raids often come in the middle of the month when there is a full moon (or 'Bombers' Moon').

14 November 1940 A formation of 449 bombers attacks the city of Coventry by night, in one of the most devastating raids of the Blitz.

December 1940–February 1941 Bad weather hampers the Luftwaffe, but the raid on London on 29 December is huge, starting over 1,400 fires in the City of London, near St Paul's Cathedral. Some people dub this 'The Second Fire of London'.

March–April 1941 There are relatively few raids on London, though one on 19 March is the worst yet, killing 750 people. Other parts of the country suffer badly, especially Glasgow, Belfast and Plymouth.

May 1941 Liverpool is blitzed for seven nights running from 1–7 May. On 10 May London has its worst raid of the entire War when 1,500 people are killed. But now, to prepare for the invasion of the Soviet Union, Hitler diverts the Luftwaffe to the east. After nine long months, the Blitz comes to an end.

When the bombing started

Britain: September 1940–May 1941

'Mum, they *are* German!' 160

This awful throb of engines 163

You could whizz around 167

The cupboard under the stairs 169

We really ought to do something 174

Sing louder! 177

'Mum, they are German!'

The first mass air raid on London came at the end of the first week of
September 1940, on the weekend before the new school term began.

Ronald McGill, returned evacuee living in Vauxhall, south London, aged 9

I wasn't frightened at all until one day it was a Saturday afternoon and
we were walking back from the Oval cricket ground. To me it was a
very vivid thing, it was aircraft and even if they were German aircraft
it was still marvellous. And the noise of the German aircraft, I couldn't
believe the noise. The sound.

My mother was so calm about this – because the sirens had gone.
She looked up and didn't think they were German. And they were tiny
glittering specks in the sun, and I said, 'Mum, they're German.'

She said, 'No they're not, they're British.'

And when you looked up it was like clouds and clouds of dancing spots
of sunlight. The whole formation had got through to London and they
were about to turn above south London and work their way down to the
docks. And only then did I realize just how many of them there were, and
that was the first time I felt any fear. And I said, 'Mum, they *are* German!'

We didn't see the bombs, we were too far away, but we saw them
curve down the Thames and we saw the great pall of smoke coming
up. Well, it was unbelievable.

Then everybody was frightened and people began to run around and
there were some cockney ladies were shaking their fists at them, and some
had knives; and you name it what they were going to do to the Germans.
They were frightened but it was a resistance fear, you know; 'You just wait
till we get our hands on you' sort of thing, rather than cowering fear.

And then we were all dragged into our shelters – we'd never used these shelters in the streets, they were just places for the children to use. But then people all poured in.

During the raid, which went on for several hours, the Luftwaffe concentrated its attack on the East End dockyards and the surrounding areas, where many poorer Londoners lived: Stepney, Whitechapel, Aldgate, Shoreditch, West Ham, Poplar and Bermondsey. That night thousands of them became homeless and 430 were killed. More than 1,000 separate fires were started – and the glow from the flames could be seen from at least 30 miles outside London.

The London fire brigade putting out fires in the East End of London during the Blitz

Oliver Bernard, Holland Park, west London, aged 14
I remember the night they set the East End alight, and the docks alight. It really was like a kind of dawn. I mean Holland Park was a long way

out of it and comparatively untouched, but from there it was like a kind of horrible dawn. It was very, very lit up.

German aircraft dropped a mixture of high-explosive bombs, designed to demolish buildings, and incendiaries, designed to start fires. Incendiary bombs were about 18 inches long and weighed about as much as a bag of sugar. They clattered down on pavements and rooftops, then burst into flames. Hundreds of them could be dropped in a single raid.

Ronald McGill

The following morning, people from the dock area – the children and the families – were all brought across to our [area]. So we had all these Bermondsey and Dockland people all around us, just sleeping where they could in shelters and things. They'd lost everything. And it really came home to us then, from that moment.

A bombed-out family sleeping in a neighbour's house

This awful throb of engines

For the following ten weeks London was bombed almost every single night, and often during the day as well. Not all the raids were as bad as that first one, though some were even worse. The East End remained one of the worst-hit areas, but central London and the City were also severely affected.

Joanna Rogers, returned evacuee, Croydon, aged 10

When the bombing started things were *much* more exciting. Daddy was very good about showing us things, letting us see things, and sometimes at night he'd say, 'Come out and look', especially when a plane was caught in a searchlight and you'd see it up there.

But we did sleep under the table most of the time because the shelter was so damp. I sometimes used to go out and look at the planes caught in the searchlights. And we were intensely patriotic and we would say, 'One of theirs!' and, 'One of ours!'

Sylvia Bell, Surbiton in Surrey, aged 5

I can remember the searchlights every night. And this awful *throb, throb, throb* of engines. But somehow I seem to remember knowing that the bombs weren't for us, that they were going to London, and we weren't quite as afraid.

Oliver Bernard

One was almost as much excited as frightened. And I remember my brother and I actually going out while raids were on and anti-aircraft guns were firing, and hearing shrapnel falling in the street – tinkling almost like glass.

Renee Bore, Poplar, east London, aged 10

I remember this funny noise going and my father gathering us all up and putting us down into the Anderson shelter. And we moaned because it smelt damp. But suddenly there was all this crashing and bashing and it sounded like thunder over and over, only much heavier and worse and it seemed to go on for a long time.

Derek Milton, Kennington, south London

[The bombs] usually came in sticks of about five or six. And you'd hear one and that would go off. And you'd hear the next one land – that'd be a bit nearer. And the next one a bit nearer. And the next one'd be over the top the other side of you. And you'd think, 'Thank Christ for that!'

Joanna Rogers

We heard bombs and we were always told if you could hear them whistling down they weren't going to fall on you – and we did hear them.

> Many people believed that whereas a bomb falling at a safe distance would be heard 'whistling' or 'screaming' as it fell, a bomb falling directly overhead would only be heard at the very last moment. The *Luftwaffe* also dropped landmines, which floated down silently on parachutes.

Renee Bore

Anyway, eventually the 'all clear' went and Father got us out and we went out the front and it seemed so strange because everybody was out there sweeping up the glass – sweeping up what remained of their windows.

> Air-raid sirens – also known as 'Whining Willies' or 'Moaning Minnies' – might sound several times a day. Everybody was drilled to recognize two sounds: the uneven wailing of the 'alert', which meant it was time to find shelter, and the steady tone of the 'all clear', which meant it was safe to come out.

Derek Milton

One shop had its windows blown in, so he boarded up the shop. He'd got one little bit of glass and put it in the middle and then underneath he wrote: 'Owing to Hitler, Our window is littler, But business goes on just the same.'

Those who only had windows broken got off relatively lightly – after just six weeks of the Blitz, more than a quarter of a million people in London were homeless. Some areas were much more badly damaged than others, but before long almost every street in the capital had at least one house missing. It became an everyday experience to see ARP wardens and heavy rescue teams clambering over the rubble in the hope of pulling out survivors. Children on their way to school were soon familiar with the smell of crushed bricks and plaster, and of gas leaking from torn pipes.

Children looking at the bomb damage caused to their school in south-east London

Derek Milton

At the end of the road there was a house got bombed. Now the one next to it wasn't touched, that was standing. But as the house went down there was a fellow in the top floor having a bath. And as the house collapsed he was left in the bath holding on to the wall of the other house by its pipes. And he suddenly looked round: no house. He was naked up there in the bath and he had to be rescued by the fire brigade.

Sylvia Limburg, central London, aged 6

I remember coming out of the shelter on the morning when our house was actually bombed. And we knew that we would never be able to go and live in it again. But just to stand there watching it burning and watching the firemen playing their hoses on it, that didn't frighten me. I knew that my mother and father were with me on the pavement. And as long as they were there it didn't matter.

A thing that did concern me was my budgie. And my father defied the wardens and managed to work his way into the house and collected a few belongings. He found his very best Homburg hat and managed to grab his razor and my budgie and a couple of pieces of my mother's special china, but not much else.

I sometimes marvel at my mother because I could see that you could quite easily lose your nerve in a situation like that, watching your house burn and all your possessions. But by that time people had just accepted that this was the kind of thing that would happen. And it happened to them. And so they'd have to pick up the pieces and carry on.

Hitler's aim in bombing British cities was to break the morale of ordinary people. He hoped they would lose the will to resist Germany and demand that the British Government surrender or make peace, but on the whole the bombing had the opposite effect, making people even more determined to defeat Germany. The day after the first big air raid, Winston Churchill had walked through the ruins in the East End, asking: 'Are we downhearted?' And there had been a huge shout of 'No!' But that was after just one day, and the Blitz would go on for nine months.

Boys salvaging wood from a London bomb site in December 1940

You could whizz around

One of the most famous images of the Blitz is of people sleeping on the platforms of the London Underground. At first, the Government didn't approve of this, because they thought it might lead to a 'deep-shelter mentality' with people refusing ever to come out! But nothing was done to stop people and eventually the Government even installed bunk-beds in some stations. Even so, only a minority of Londoners chose this option. Most used household shelters or didn't bother with a shelter at all.

On the tube station platforms, there was often quite a squash, especially at rush hour when people were still trying to get home from work. But after 10.30 pm the trains stopped and the live rail was switched off, so some people even slept between the tracks.

Richard Faint, Lambeth, south London, aged 14
We used to sleep every night in Lambeth North Underground station. And we each had our own place, and we used to put the bedding down and that was it for the night.

167

Renee Bore

You'd have people saying, 'Well I slept there last night, that was my space.' And you'd say, 'It hasn't got your *name* on it.'

Richard Faint

We used to have a great time, all the kids. We used to get up to various games. We used to enjoy it. There was a sort of mini-canteen there, the lady made tea and cakes. And of course everybody knew everybody, all the neighbours, all the people in the area. And then the last train used to come through and we used to settle down for the night until the early hours of the morning.

Families sheltering in Piccadilly Circus Underground station in central London

Ronald McGill

I can remember doing homework in there in the evenings. We were there for weeks in the big long period of the Blitz. All the children used to work and do their homework on the station. And that was where we did our schooling.

Renee Bore

You could whizz around on the underground providing your mother let you go. Let's face it, as poor children, we didn't [usually] go on the underground, so that was our introduction.

Richard Faint

You'd come up in the morning and you'd see the devastation. [If] there'd been an air raid the night before you would come up and wonder what you would see, or still see, sort of standing and not standing.

> Tube stations were not as safe as people thought. High-explosive bombs could penetrate up to 50 feet through solid ground and there were several disasters. In October 1940, 68 people were killed when a bomb hit Balham station, and in January 1941 Bank station was hit, killing 56 people. But the worst incident came later in the War, on 3 March 1943, when a panic at Bethnal Green station resulted in a stampede in which 178 people died.

The cupboard under the stairs

In the first period of the Blitz London had been the prime target, but after a few weeks the attacks began to widen and almost every major town and city in Britain eventually had its own experience of being blitzed. The Luftwaffe had not finished with London, but now it was just one of many places likely to be targeted on a given night.

Inge Engelhard, German Jewish refugee in Coventry, aged 10

Suddenly it started and almost every night there'd be raids. If the raids lasted over a certain amount of hours, we didn't have to go to school. And the next day, children would come into school and say, 'Oh we've been bombed' or another one would say, 'No, we haven't, not yet.' And people were very brave and very optimistic.

Children in Coventry search for books in their bombed school

Sylvia Parkes, an evacuee in Chasetown, Staffordshire, near Birmingham, aged 13

I used to sleep in the cupboard under the stairs with the old dog. And you'd lay there at night and the floor would be jumping up and down beneath you. Rex would come padding out of the dining room and cuddle up with me in this cupboard. He was company because it was a little scary under there in the dark all on your own with this jarring going on and this funny sound, rumblings and bangings and whatnot.

Inge Engelhard

On the night of the [Coventry] Blitz the house more or less fell on top of us, except we'd just got out in time and ran across the road. And all night I was worried about my brother, who'd broken his leg a few weeks previously looking for incendiary bombs and he fell into a hole. And in the morning, there wasn't even an all-clear left to sound the all-clear, there was no siren left. Coventry was badly, badly damaged.

The Coventry Blitz was on 14 November 1940, when the city suffered one of the worst raids of all. Fifty thousand buildings over 100 acres of the city centre were destroyed, and 568 people killed. A third of the city's houses and half of its buses were wrecked. The Nazis even coined a new word for the total destruction of a foreign city: 'Coventration'.

Sylvia Parkes

When I stayed with Uncle Bill we used to sit on the stile at night and watch the bombers going over in the searchlights and watch the bullets and various things flying around like a sort of glorified firework display, and the fires over Birmingham. The stile used to literally shake with the weight of the bombing. And on the night they dropped a stick of bombs in Chasetown itself, they come whistling down past us and we just sort of ducked. There was a dirty great bang and we got up and sat on the stile again. It all seemed so natural somehow. You never seemed to think about what might happen in the next minute. You were still alive, so you got up again. That was it.

In cities outside London there were no tube stations to shelter in, but open countryside was easier to reach and people often chose to sleep there rather than risk staying at home. When Plymouth was blitzed in April 1941, around 50,000 residents – including many whose houses had already been hit – trekked into the surrounding countryside at night and slept in fields.

Arthur Dales, from Hull, aged 15

We could hear the aircraft coming over and then we would count – *one … two … three … four … five* – as you heard the scream of the bombs. And the shelter was rocking. The guns at the back of us were firing non-stop so the noise was tremendous. And I thought my mother was getting a little bit worried and I knew she was religious so I said to her, 'What is the 23rd Psalm, then? I think that's appropriate.' So she recited the 23rd Psalm ['The Lord Is My Shepherd'] and I said, 'Oh yes, I wondered what it was.'

Eric Hill, Southampton, aged 8

We were in the bottom part of Southampton with my mother when the air-raid sirens blew, and we had to dive for cover. I remember we were in this air-raid shelter for about three or four hours and when we came out the High Street was running with melted margarine and butter because they'd hit the cold storage [depot].

Maria Siegel, German Jewish refugee living in Sevenoaks, Kent, aged 15

In due course, the school was bombed. We were all sitting after our evening meal, knitting blankets for the troops in Finland or something. And suddenly there was this enormous bang. The headmistress's husband shouted, 'Get on the floor!'

I remember getting all tangled up in everybody's wool but finding a place and lying down. And my good friend Ursula decided on the same bit of ground and fell on top of me. And I must confess I thought: 'Good, if the house comes down, it comes down on *her* first and *I'll* live.' That's awful – I *liked* Ursula – but that's how I felt.

Ronald McGill in Vauxhall

It was the night bombing that took the toll of people. You didn't get proper sleep. And I can remember my dad – after Christmas – taking me to the very top floor of our house. And we were near enough to see the City burning. He put my feet on his shoulders and lifted me up and told me to look at this and to see this, and remember it all your life. And it was just a red sea – with chimney pots. Unbelievable.

The raid on the City of London (the area around St Paul's Cathedral) took place on 29 December 1940. That night a total of 2,300 fire pumps were in action in the area, whereas before the War there were only 1,850 pumps available across the whole of Britain. Miraculously St Paul's Cathedral survived undamaged, though bombs fell all around it. Thanks to dramatic photographs of the dome rising through the smoke, it soon became a powerful symbol of hope and defiance in Britain.

St Paul's Cathedral during the bombing raid of 29 December 1940

Bombs did not always explode on impact, and sometimes an unexploded bomb (UXB) would lie buried in a street for days or even weeks before it was noticed.

Gwendoline Watts, returned evacuee, Birmingham, aged 14

My mother had gone to London, and I was looking after Helen and Jack. So we three children were in the shelter – my father was out on the street fire-watching. He would come back every half hour or so to see that we were all right. And I said, 'Dad, there's a bomb dropped near here, it's in the garden.'

And they all looked round our garden but there was nothing there.

I said, 'There is.' I could feel it. Something had come into the ground. They looked and looked and couldn't find it. Then my mother came back and Dad said, 'Take the children to the seaside for a few days, give them a break.' So we went to Rhyl.

We were in Rhyl for three or four days – nice and quiet – [then] we came back. We were walking down Foxton Road and we said, 'Those houses are missing.' There was bomb damage and it was right opposite our house – our windows were blown out. And Dad said, 'Yes, you said there was an unexploded bomb.' I'd felt the vibrations in our garden, it was right opposite there. I knew something had happened.

 By the end of November 1940, there were 3,000 unexploded bombs dotted around London waiting to be defused. Some remained undiscovered until long after the War.

We really ought to do something

Teenage boys who wanted to get closer to the action sometimes volunteered to work as messengers for the local fire services or ARP wardens' post. With many phone lines down, communications were often stretched to

breaking point, and the emergency services relied on messenger boys –
usually on bicycles (and later motorcycles) – to keep in touch during and
after air raids.

Arthur Dales, ARP wardens' messenger boy, Hull, aged 15
I thought it was time something was done about the war situation. I had
a friend, and we were coming up to 16 and I said, 'Well we really ought
to do something about this.' And we joined the messenger service.

Graham Swain, Fire Service messenger boy, Bournemouth, aged 16
When the sirens went and everybody took shelter, we belted on our
bikes to the fire station. And whenever an appliance went out to a fire,
one of these cycle messengers would hare after it to report back 'so
many pumps required' or 'incident over' or that sort of thing.

Fire Service dispatch riders

During the Blitz, thousands of volunteer firemen worked alongside the ordinary peacetime fire brigade as 'auxiliaries'. Schools and church halls were used as temporary fire stations.

Stan Poole, Fire Service messenger boy, north London, aged 14

Sometimes you would help a bloke on the [water] jets, because those jets were so powerful it took maybe two or three blokes to hold it down.

Lawrence Beaumont, ARP wardens' messenger boy, Hull, aged 15

The most thing you had to bother about was incendiaries, stray incendiaries. You usually sandbagged them – there were always plenty of sandbags around. You just smother them, put the sandbag on top and leave it. There was quite a few of them … dozens. On the roads, sometimes on the roofs. I was quite good at climbing.

Stan Poole

On Tottenham Court Road there used to be a big firm [of] outfitters. And there was fire-bombs dropped on it. Two of us went upstairs and it was fire everywhere and fire coming through the windows. And we tried to find our way up.

We get to another floor and there's an air-raid warden trying on suits. The place is on fire and he's in front of these mirrors trying on suits for himself!

Anyway, we went up on the roof and there were incendiary bombs laying about. And we didn't have a bucket, we didn't have sand … nothing. But we got hold of shovels somehow, and we're shovelling these blazing incendiary bombs and chucking them into Tottenham Court Road, the two of us.

And voices shouts out, 'Stop that!'

And they got an answer; 'What do they want, to burn the place down? Are they going to wait for a fire-brigade pump?' So we were shovelling this stuff over.

Arthur Dales

We usually had a few minutes from the time the warning sounded to the time the first aircraft came over. I got on my bike and I was just going along Salisbury Street when the [anti-aircraft] barrage opened up and I could hear this German aircraft – he seemed very low. So I speeded up, bent over the handlebars, and my dynamo headlamp fanned out in front of me with such a beam of light, I thought, 'Crikey, he'll see me.' Anyway I got to the warden's post and the air-raid warden in charge said, 'Come on, get inside quick. You don't want to be out in this lot!'

Sing louder!

Despite the bombs, everyday life had to continue somehow – whether it was doing the shopping, going to school or getting to work. (At that time most children left school and took their first jobs between the ages of 14 and 16.) Children had little choice but to adapt to the circumstances.

Gwendoline Watts

My father painted the inside of the shelter, and he'd got little butterflies painted on the walls. He had a stove down there. He built bunk beds on either side for us because he was always out fire-watching. It was really a little home from home, so that as soon as we'd had our meal we'd go straight down with our books and knitting, whatever we were doing. So that became a way of life: home, have a meal, down the shelter.

Fire watchers were responsible for spotting incendiaries before they had a chance to cause full-scale fires. They often sat on top of tall buildings where they could more easily survey blacked-out cities. Most men who had not yet been drafted into the armed services spent at least some evenings on duty, either with the Home Guard, or as an ARP warden, an auxiliary fireman or a fire watcher. Many women also did these jobs.

An ARP warden at her post

Edward Butt, returned evacuee, West Ham, east London, aged 10
When the siren went we'd go down the shelter. But you left your front
door open just in case there was an incendiary bomb at the back of
the house and the fire watchers could just run through. Parents would
make the cushions look presentable because somebody might come
through. That was taboo, to have an untidy house. And the last thing
Mother did before she went down to the shelter was to just bump up
the cushions and put it all straight.

Renee Bore

My mother was a very nervy person anyway. She heard that an Anderson shelter had got a direct hit, so she lost faith in it. So we then went to a little church round the corner, and we used to go into their crypt and they used to have one of those [portable] toilets with a curtain round it, and every time one of the women went in, we used to have to sing to cover the noise. We used to think, 'God, Mrs So-and-So's in there – *sing louder!*'

Gwendoline Watts

The next morning there'd be incendiaries everywhere and you'd have to pick your way through the rubble. The trams weren't running but, no matter what happened, you had to get to work. I had to walk through the city centre as best I could – with everybody else – going round craters, stepping over hosepipes. Chaos everywhere, the smell of burning. And even if you arrived at your office at 11 o'clock they were still pleased to see you.

Sylvia Bell, from Surbiton, aged 5

I can remember going to school and saying goodbye to mother and not knowing if I was going to see her when I came home, whether she'd still be there. And the sirens went while I was on my way. And we always had to go straight to the shelters. We were told. And I didn't want to do that, I wanted to get to school, because though I didn't much care for school I felt I'd be safer at school than I would be in a shelter.

I don't think we did any lessons because we spent most of the time in the shelters singing 'Ten Green Bottles' and 'One Man Went To Mow'. I can remember the teacher – as you could hear the guns getting louder and the bombs falling – he would urge us to sing louder and you'd be singing loudly and listening at the same time and wondering if the bomb was coming for you. And I can remember the drip, drip, drip of the water running down the walls in the shelter. All very cold and wet and frightening.

Derek Milton

Anybody who says they weren't frightened, they're lying, because once the sirens go your stomach used to turn over and you'd get a feeling of dread, you know, 'Here it comes again.' But I never saw anybody openly show it. Everybody sort of gritted their teeth and tried to appear, 'Oh yes, coming over again are they?' That kind of attitude.

As the Blitz went on people became more likely to take chances. For example, although many people had stopped going to the cinema at the beginning of the Blitz, audiences gradually returned and even stayed put during raids. Cinemas were by no means safe, and during the War 60 of them were bomb-damaged in London alone. But the latest American films – including *Gone With The Wind* and Walt Disney's *Pinocchio* – were a distraction from constant air raids, and at least helped to drown out the noise. Some cinemas even offered all-night feature films and a communal sing-along.

Oliver Bernard

A lot of people seemed to me very cheerful and incredibly sort of brave and happy really, considering what was going on. One thought of peace and that it would be a great relief from all this very tiring business, because it was tiring to be kept awake night after night or to hear air-raid sirens punctually at nightfall. It was tiring. But it wasn't depressing.

The nine-month Blitz killed about 43,000 British civilians and seriously injured many more. About two million houses were either destroyed or badly damaged and one in six Londoners became homeless at some point. Even so, the destruction was not nearly as bad as in German and Japanese cities later in the War. (The single Allied air raid on the German city of Dresden in February 1945 killed at least 35,000 people and some estimate that the figure may be more than three times that. On 9–10 March 1945 American bombers raided Tokyo, the Japanese capital, killing around 100,000 people.)

The 'Final Solution'

June 1941 Hitler launches a massive invasion of the Soviet Union. As they advance inside the country the Germans set up a few ghettos (including Riga, Kovno and Vilna), but now they simply round up most Jews (along with Communists) and shoot them. These mass executions mark the beginning of the Nazis' systematic murder of Jews.

16 October 1941 The Nazis begin to send German Jews to the ghettos in Poland and Russia. They want to make Germany 'Jew-free'.

2 December 1941 German troops have penetrated hundreds of miles into the Soviet Union and now reach the outskirts of Moscow, the capital city. By now there are about eight million Jews in the territory under their control.

7 December 1941 Japanese planes launch a surprise attack on the United States naval base at Pearl Harbor in Hawaii. The following day the US declares war on Japan and three days later Germany declares war on the US. The War is now being fought around the globe.

20 January 1942 Senior Nazi officials meet at a lakeside villa in Wannsee, near Berlin. Hitler has asked them for a 'Final Solution to the Jewish Question'. The Nazis have already shot hundreds of thousands of people in Poland and the Soviet Union, and killed many others through starvation and disease in the ghettos, or by working them to death in labour camps. At Wannsee, they make detailed plans for the murder of every single Jewish man, woman and child in Europe.

Spring 1942 Deep in the Polish countryside, the Nazis build several new camps – not 'labour camps' or 'concentration camps' this time, but 'death camps'. Fitted with gas chambers – sealed rooms where people can be packed inside and then overcome with poisonous gas – the camps are designed for the single purpose of killing those who are sent to them. The Nazis build these camps at Sobibor, Treblinka and Belzec. They also turn the concentration camp at Chelmno into another death camp and install gas chambers at Majdanek and Auschwitz concentration camps.

Summer 1942 The Nazis begin to empty the ghettos they have created in Poland by sending their inhabitants in batches to the new death camps. Meanwhile, Jews in France, Holland, Belgium, Slovakia, Rumania and Croatia are forced to wear the Star of David badge. No ghettos are set up in these countries, but soon Jews are being rounded up and sent to Auschwitz.

June 1943 The Nazis order the complete destruction – or 'liquidation' – of the ghettos in Poland and the Soviet Union. All Jews remaining inside are to be sent to the death camps. By the end of the year the Polish ghettos are almost completely empty and the Jewish population of Poland has been virtually wiped out. Their job done, the Nazis close down most of the death camps. However, the biggest of them – Auschwitz – operates until almost the very end of the War, as the Nazis continue to round up Jews from all corners of Europe.

Taken away

Poland: 1941–1943

A fair amount of disappearing 184
We couldn't believe it 187
'To the right! To the left!' 189
Heroic things 193

A fair amount of disappearing

Hitler had raged against the Jews of Europe for years and even predicted their 'annihilation' in the event of war. But few had taken him at his word, unable to imagine murder on such a scale. Even Hitler may not have really believed it possible until the shootings in the Soviet Union showed him what his Nazi followers were prepared to do, and what he could get away with. But now that Germany's military victories had given him almost complete control of mainland Europe, who was there to stop him?

The Nazis soon began rounding up Jews wherever they could find them and forcibly sending them east (a process known as 'deportation'). The first to be deported in this way were those from Greater Germany itself, the ones who had lived under Nazi rule since the very beginning.

Ruth Heilbron, deported in 1941, from Germany to the Riga Ghetto in Latvia, then part of the Soviet Union, aged 18
The journey was horrendous. It took either three days and four nights or four days and three nights, I can't remember. We had hardly any sanitations, we had a bucket which overflowed. There was no water, they didn't give us any water. The further we came east, the colder it got. The windows froze over. We were not allowed to open the windows. The doors were bolted. And the windows froze over, so we didn't even know where we were.

Then suddenly the train stopped, the doors were pulled open and outside they shouted, *'Raus! Raus!'* which means 'Out! Out!' We were stiff, we could hardly walk because it was by that time minus 20 degrees. And lots of people got frostbites, couldn't walk.

The SS came in with their big dogs and truncheons and were herding us out of the railway trains. And there we stood, on the side of a goods train outside Riga. The wind was howling and the ice was in the road and snow. And we had to get in rows of five, [and] we had to march towards Riga Ghetto.

SS men with rifles and truncheons and big dogs were accompanying us, and with loud-hailers they were saying: 'Who is not able to walk, old people and mothers with children, you will have to have it comfortable. You don't have to walk any further, there are some vans waiting for you. You go on to these lorries and you'll meet your loved ones soon again.' But later on, after the War, I found out that these lorries were portable gas chambers.

> From 1941, SS 'Action Groups' began to use special vans to kill people at some concentration camps and ghettos, including Riga. The vans were designed so that the poisonous exhaust from the engine was pumped back inside. People were told they were being moved from one place to another, loaded on to the vans and then suffocated as they drove off.

In 1941 few people outside Poland and the Soviet Union could imagine what was going on there, let alone what the Nazis were planning. Jews sent to the east were told they were being 'resettled'. Neither they, nor the rest of the population, knew that most of them were being sent to their deaths. But as time went on the truth began to emerge, and more and more Jews in countries outside Poland and the Soviet Union came to live in daily fear of round-ups by the Gestapo.

Peter Frank, in Prague, Greater Germany (formerly Czechoslovakia), aged 12

The great danger was curfew; you never went out anywhere near the curfew if you had any sense in case you got stuck there. You didn't go anywhere near the places which were the principal German sites, like the palace where the Gestapo was. I lived very near the broadcasting station. I made absolutely sure that I crossed the road away from the station, well away on to the other pavement, then made my way quickly past it. If there were Germans anywhere, you didn't gawp, you went away. There was a fair amount of crossing of streets or disappearing into a house, or if you were in the main town, into passages. There are a lot of passages from one street to another in Prague, so you could disappear that way.

> A number of Jews throughout occupied Europe chose to live in hiding rather than risk deportation. One of the best-known cases is that of Anne Frank in Holland. Holland had been occupied since 1940, and by the summer of 1942 Dutch Jews had been forced to wear the Star of David badge. On 6 July 1942, as the first deportations to Poland got underway, 13-year-old Anne Frank and her parents went into hiding in Amsterdam. In a small secret flat in the attic of the building where her father had his office, they lived together with four other people for more than two years, never setting foot outside. There, Anne wrote her famous diary, published after the War. In August 1944 the whole group was betrayed to the Gestapo, arrested and sent to Auschwitz. Anne's father Otto was the only one to survive the War.

Inside the ghettos in Poland, conditions naturally became worse than ever as newcomers began to arrive from Greater Germany. The Nazis dealt with the population increase with their usual methods.

Kitty Felix, Lublin Ghetto

Worst of all was the overcrowding, because they began bringing in thousands of people, people who couldn't speak the language. They couldn't communicate with the local population, they had nowhere to live. At least we could speak the language, and we could still find accommodation because my father had some possessions that he could barter with. But you had people who came in from different countries, who simply couldn't do this. They had no means of earning a living or finding food.

Josef Perl, deported from Czechoslovakia to Poland, aged 11

After ten minutes walk into the ghetto, I saw a column, five abreast, of naked people, women, men, children, old people, young people. After the column went past me for five minutes, [the SS guard] ordered me to stop. He asked me to undress and he pushed me into the column. We marched and we marched, we marched into a forest where a huge long ditch was already dug. I could hear *tat-tat-tat-tat-tat-tat* – a machine gun going. But when you don't see it, it doesn't bother you. It's far away, it doesn't somehow connect with anything. But as you come nearer and nearer you begin to see faces, so you know who is being killed.

All of a sudden, I must have been about five or six rows from the front, I saw my mother and my four sisters lined up and before I had a chance to say 'Mother' they were already dead.

■ ■ ■ ■ ■

We couldn't believe it

Soon the Nazis began the process of emptying the ghettos by sending batches of people to their newly built death camps – usually in trainloads of three or four thousand at a time. At first, they tried to keep the death camps a secret from the inmates of the ghettos, since they knew they would have much more trouble rounding people up for deportation if those people knew where they were going. So the Nazis told them they were being 'relocated' or 'resettled' somewhere better.

Most people were sceptical, but it was hard to imagine anywhere worse than the ghettos, so some allowed themselves to be persuaded. And even when rumours of the camps got back to the ghettos people were still reluctant to believe them.

A group of Jews is marched under guard through a Polish town

Edyta Klein, Warsaw Ghetto

The whole ghetto had posters that we were going to be evacuated east and the only people allowed to stay in the ghetto would be the ones that work in factories.

Roman Halter, Lodz Ghetto

The Germans were selling tickets and saying, 'Come on, pay me so much and you will be the first on this cattle train.' And people believed that, because one wants to believe that life exists – they did not want to feel that they are going to an extermination camp.

Residents of the Lodz Ghetto began to be deported to Chelmno in January 1942. The first train left the Warsaw Ghetto for Treblinka on 22 July. Around 5,000 people followed from Warsaw every day for the next two months, reducing the population of the ghetto from 360,000 to 65,000.

Janina Dawidowicz, Warsaw Ghetto

I think at first people didn't know. We were told we were [being] resettled in the east. I don't think that any addresses were given. People were told that they were going to some sort of labour camps. Some people maintained that they had received postcards from the people who have gone saying, 'We have arrived well. Waiting for you to come.' But about halfway through the actual liquidation of the ghetto, which was in late summer 1942, some people escaped from Treblinka, came back to the Warsaw Ghetto and warned us. I remember listening to this man. I saw him. He came to our house. And not everybody believed him. Some people simply said, 'Poor man, something must have happened to him, panic monger. It can't be. It just can't be. It's never happened in the world, things like that. You don't just take thousands of people and gas them.'

Edyta Klein

I remember that as children we would play, and from bits and pieces of cardboard or fabric we would try to recreate what the gas chamber … what it looked like. But mainly we couldn't. We couldn't believe it. We couldn't believe that anything like that existed.

'To the right! To the left!'

Each time a deportation train was due to depart, people were 'selected' to go on it. This was usually done by lining everybody up for inspection and picking people out. Since the Nazis wanted to keep their factories going until the very last minute, the people most likely to be selected for deportation were the elderly, the ill, and children who were too young to work.

Of all the cruelties inflicted on people by the Nazis, perhaps the worst of all were these 'selections'. With no more than a flick of the wrist, an SS soldier could condemn one person to death, whilst letting their neighbour live. In an instant, mothers and fathers were separated from children, brothers from sisters, husbands from wives. One group was taken straight to the death camps and never seen again, while the other had to return to the misery of the ghetto – until the next selection.

Worse still, perhaps, was the way the Nazis often forced members of the Jewish councils to make the selections themselves, which meant condemning their own friends and neighbours to certain death.

Ryvka Berkowicz, Zdunska Wola Ghetto, Poland, aged 10

Rumours circulated that children and old people were not safe so we took my grandparents and one younger cousin who was only about three or four and we hid them in the attic. The rest of us walked into the street which was already crowded with people. We didn't know where to go, so we just followed one another. Then we came to a very big field surrounded by Gestapo, SS and with the big dogs, big guard dogs. They waited a while until everybody was together and then they started giving orders over the loudspeakers. The first was that everybody should sit down so that they could overlook us better and the [next] order they gave was that parents should hand over all their children up to 18 years of age. The cries from the mothers, 'Almighty God, help us.' It's still ringing in my ears. You could soon see the children running towards the officers, little ones, bigger ones, the bigger ones holding their young siblings in their arms. While all this was going on my mother was trying to hide me on one side, and my sister on the other side.

Roman Halter

Then, 1942, where the selection took place in the Lodz Ghetto, my sister and her two children were taken, at least the children were taken and she said, 'Leave me my children.' And they said no. So she went with the children. It was quite obvious that whoever is going to be taken away is going to be taken somewhere where they are going to be murdered. I was selected together with my mother and we were on a cart because we were living in an area where there were narrow passages and lorries could not get there. And during the selection, because we looked so starved, both she and I were taken. My mother had swollen legs from hunger and she said, 'Although you are thin, you are able to run. When I tell you, *"Run!"*, take off your wooden clogs, jump off and run in a zig-zag way and then climb up over the outer bog and over the fence.' And I did this, and although they shouted '*Halt! Halt!*' somehow I wasn't noticed. And I jumped over the other side and they thought I had jumped in the mire. So the SS [guard] fired a few bullets into the bog and then he went back to the convoy.

On 5 August 1942, SS soldiers arrived at one of the orphanages in the Warsaw Ghetto. They had come to 'resettle' its 200 children. The orphanage's director, 64-year-old Janusz Korczak, was a popular Polish educator and writer who had spent his life speaking up for children's rights in Poland. Because of his fame, he had received several offers from people willing to help him escape but he had turned them all down, believing that it was his duty to stay with the children in his care. When the Nazis came to take the children from the orphanage they offered Korczak and the other orphanage staff the opportunity to remain in the ghetto, but none of them accepted. So that they would be less afraid, Korczak walked in front of the children as they made their way to the train station that day. They all died at Treblinka.

Edyta Klein

Every few weeks a thousand people would get out of the courtyard, 700 would go back. Sometimes more, sometimes less. And the three of us, my mother, my stepfather and myself, survived all the selections. I don't know how. At one time I could see the chances are so minimal.

Because you always stand in rows of five, and then: 'To the right!' – you can go back to the factory. 'To the left!' – it was the vans would take you away. I realized that standing three in a row of five that there are practically no chances of all of us coming through. And I pushed my mother to the front and I pushed my stepfather to the back. I can't even remember whom did I push out in their place. And we all of us went to the selection. We all survived. I can't remember who those people were, or if they ever survived. By pushing them, did I push them closer to their death?

Jewish men, women and children are rounded up in the Warsaw Ghetto

Alicia Gornowski, aged 14 in 1940 at formation of Warsaw Ghetto
[The Jewish police] were chosen to keep order but afterwards [they] had to select people and they had to bring a set quota [number] of people to the Germans to be sent away. I understand now that they had to do it because they had to save their own skin. If they didn't bring enough people they and their family would be taken first. The way

it was done was very cruel, they were taking children from mothers. I've seen it, it was very dramatic. People became animals because life was so difficult.

> One of the most infamous members of the Jewish councils was Chaim Rumkowski, leader of the Lodz Ghetto. Nicknamed 'King Chaim', he was notorious for his apparent readiness to carry out selections for the Nazis. He argued that refusal to give the Nazis what they wanted would only lead to punishment for everybody, so when the Germans ordered a huge 'resettlement' of people under ten years old and over 65, Rumkowski made a speech, urging people to 'give me your children'. 'We have to accept this evil order,' he said. 'I have to take away the children because otherwise others will also be taken.'

Heroic things

People have sometimes wondered why there was not more resistance to the Nazis from the people living in the ghettos. Why didn't people fight back? In fact, there were revolts in a number of ghettos, including Warsaw. But putting up a fight was much easier said than done.

Berek Obuchowski, Ozorkow, Poland, aged 11
I don't remember seeing any heroic things because, as everybody realized, as soon as one raised a hand – even as much as raised a hand – against a German, they would automatically take a hundred people. It would mean nothing to them to take a hundred people into the square and just shoot them for fun. If there was one amongst us who wanted to take revenge or try and be a hero, the other people would object because they would know that a lot of innocent people would be harmed, injured or killed.

Janina Dawidowicz

Also there is apathy. One of the reasons why people didn't fight sooner was that when you're starving you're too apathetic. When you're so swollen that you can hardly keep your eyes open, that you can hardly see and you can't move, how are you going to fight?

> In January 1943, Heinrich Himmler (the SS leader) ordered the final 'liquidation' of the Warsaw Ghetto. This meant the deportation of its remaining 65,000 Jews – mostly men still working in the factories. But when SS soldiers entered the ghetto to round people up they met with stiff resistance from fighters armed with mostly home-made weapons. On 19 April 1943 the Germans entered the ghetto in force, using tanks and heavy artillery to destroy it street by street. Even then the Jewish resistance held out for almost a month until the ghetto was completely destroyed. Those not killed in the fighting were either shot or deported to Treblinka.

■■■■■

Auschwitz 1940–1944

May–June 1940 On the outskirts of the small Polish town of Oswiecim, which the Germans rename Auschwitz, the Nazis set up a large concentration camp. At first it is used only as a prison camp for Jews and other Poles, and is just one of a network of similar camps throughout Germany and Poland.

Spring 1941 The Nazis install German factories and chemical plants in Auschwitz, close to the concentration camp. They use prisoners from the camp to supply the workforce.

September 1941 As an 'experiment', the Nazis lock several hundred Soviet prisoners of war into a large room at Auschwitz and drop poison gas through the roof, killing them all.

October 1941 The Nazis enlarge the camp significantly. It is now a vast complex of wooden and brick huts surrounded by electrified barbed-wire fences and watchtowers. Over the main gate hangs a sign bearing the words 'Arbeit Macht Frei' – 'Work Brings Freedom'.

Spring 1942 The Nazis have decided on their 'Final Solution' and Auschwitz has been fitted with several makeshift gas chambers. While the main part of the camp continues to operate as a concentration camp supplying workers for the factories, the other part is given over to murder. Thanks to its convenient position and good railway connections, Auschwitz becomes the hub of the Final Solution. The Nazis are soon bringing people not only from the ghettos in the east, but also from countries all over occupied Europe – beginning with Holland, Belgium and France.

October 1942 All Jews held in concentration camps in Germany are now sent to Auschwitz. Two months later, most remaining Gypsies in countries under German occupation are sent there.

March 1943 The Nazis install a new set of larger, purpose-built gas chambers, shielded from the rest of the camp behind a screen of tall trees. By the end of the year, most of the other death camps in Poland have closed down, but Auschwitz is becoming increasingly busy.

September 1943 Germany's ally Italy has not so far co-operated with Hitler in sending its Jews to Poland. Now Allied troops land in the south, and Hitler orders German troops to occupy northern Italy. As a result, thousands of Italian Jews are sent to Auschwitz.

Spring 1944 The Nazis build an extension to the main railway line leading to Auschwitz, so that trains can run directly to the gas chambers without stopping at the main camp. Nearly half a million Hungarian Jews are taken from their homes and sent there. By the end of the year, when the camp is dismantled, over a million people have been murdered there.

If the trees could talk

Auschwitz: 1942–1944

A distant red glow   198

'How nice to be so kind'   200

Everything was taken from you   202

Some way of survival   205

A huge pile of jumble   207

'What shall I do? Where shall I be?'   210

You simply thought of yourself   212

A distant red glow

From 1942 until almost the very end of the War, the railway system across Europe was extremely busy. Not only were the Nazis transporting vital weapons and supplies to front-line soldiers in the east (and later in the west), they were also transporting Jews and Gypsies from all over Europe to the gas chambers in Poland. This task seems to have been every bit as important to them as trying to win the War.

Arrival at Auschwitz

In ghettos in the east, and in concentration camps and transit camps across Europe, SS guards packed people inside trains designed for transporting cattle. Then the doors were sealed and the trains departed on journeys that could sometimes last for days.

Roman Halter, deported from Lodz Ghetto to Auschwitz in 1944, aged 17

We were put on the train – I mean, into the cattle truck – and it was locked. And we set off, and inside there were buckets in the corner, very little air. You could sip in air through the chinks in the walls. There were tiny little windows up on top, horizontal slits which were criss-crossed with barbed wire. So some people would stand on one another's shoulder in order to get air from there.

The train shunted, stopped, went on, shunted, stopped. Soon the buckets were full and some people fainted and lay on the floor and others sat on them and the whole place stunk. And we were still nowhere near our destination.

Barbara Stimler, deported from Lodz Ghetto to Auschwitz 1943, aged 16

Before we got into the train they gave us all a loaf of bread, and in the middle of the train was a barrel of water, and of course they put us in and we were like sardines. And I still did not know where they were taking us. I just did not know that a place like Auschwitz existed.

The journey took about, I don't know, 12 hours, I don't know how long. But the stench in this train, and people fainting. It was just… You cannot describe… Unless you lived through it, it's indescribable. And two young women there, they took a bit of sugar and they were giving into my mouth this bit of sugar to keep me alive.

■ ■ ■ ■ ■

Many people would have heard rumours about Auschwitz and some probably feared the worst. But as the trains approached the enormous camp gates, few could have guessed what sort of world they were about to enter.

Kitty Felix, captured after escape from Lublin Ghetto, sent to Auschwitz in 1943, aged 17

When we arrived in the very early hours we approached an area surrounded by fences that was lit up. And the first thing that actually struck us was a kind of glow in the distance, a distant red glow and a peculiar smell.

Barbara Stimler

We couldn't understand. The place was lighted up. What is this chimney burning night and day? And flame is coming out and the camp is absolutely lighted up.

■ ■ ■ ■ ■

'How nice to be so kind'

The first thing that happened to most people on arrival at the camp was a 'selection'. Camp prisoners, who wore striped uniforms that looked like pyjamas, helped unload the trains and organize people into lines for inspection by SS officers. From each trainload of arrivals, the fittest and strongest would be picked out to work in the labour camp. The rest – mostly women, young children and the elderly – would soon be dead.

Roman Halter

When the wagons were opened and they were shouting that we have to get out, hardly anybody moved because we were sort of one mass of people. Then the SS came up, shouted, *'Raus! Raus!'* [Out! Out!], but still people didn't move. And then the men with pyjamas jumped in and said, 'Leave everything behind, just get out. Get out!' And people started falling out – it's quite a height from the top of a cattle truck to the ground.

Barbara Stimler

We had to get off the trains, and they said leave your luggage. Now they start sorting. The men separate, and the women separate. There's screams from the mothers who were separated from their children. And of course they had the bats and they start beating and all this. It was just terrible.

We started going through a gate and then the two girls are still giving me this sugar to keep me alive. I still don't know where I am. One woman goes to the left, one to the right. I am going with these girls to the right. They start counting us. Counting us and counting us.

A 'selection' soon after arrival at Auschwitz

Franz Brichta, arrived in Auschwitz 1944, aged 16

We were put into lines six abreast. I was with my mother but somehow I lost her. But she spotted me and walked towards me, shook my hand

and walked away again. We were taken in front of somebody who would point right and left and again we obviously didn't know what it was all about. There were lorries waiting, and those who were ill or crippled or old were told they could get on this lorry and we thought, 'How nice to be so kind.'

Anyway, I'd seen my mother go first and she walked to the left. I'm never really with it, I'm a bit slow on the uptake, so when my turn came I walked forward, didn't take much notice of the men in front and simply followed where my mother had gone, to the left. But I was called back and turned to the right.

Everything was taken from you

Those whom the Nazis sent to the left went directly to the gas chambers, though they did not know that was where they were going since the chambers were disguised as communal shower rooms. People were told to undress before stepping inside. Then the doors were locked and canisters of cyanide gas were dropped inside.

Those sent to the right went to the main labour camp for registration. There SS guards confiscated any personal possessions that people had managed to cling on to. Every last reminder of normal life was now removed.

Tauba Biber, arrived in Auschwitz 1943, aged 18

We were stripped of everything, our hair shaved off, and taken into this shower. And there was a friend of mine with a mother and with a sister. They couldn't even recognize each other. We were given those striped dresses, and we marched and marched again, till we got into a barrack. There were barracks, maybe 1,000 women in one barrack. With just a blanket and bunks.

Barbara Stimler

They took us to a place where they shaved us. I was a young girl, I was 15. To look like a monster, without hair. We didn't recognize each other. They shaved us and they start giving us dresses, just dresses, no shoes. They put us in a barrack where we had bunks, five girls to a bunk.

Young women in the camp at Auschwitz

Kitty Felix

We were taken into a large hall where you were completely stripped. Everything was taken off you, from you, you were totally naked. You were shaved and you were smeared with a sort of green fluid [disinfectant] and then you were taken to a next hall where you were given – well at least we were given – uniforms. So everyone was issued with a jacket and trousers and a pair of clogs. We were taken to another hall where we were tattooed on our left forearms. And my mother was tattooed first, her number was 39933, and I was tattooed immediately afterwards, 39934.

After that we were taken to a barrack, or what was known as a block. And of course having arrived too late to receive any food whatsoever, we didn't receive a single bread ration, or anything to drink [until the next day].

I had no idea what I was actually there for, all I knew is I am here and I am going to fight for my life. And from that point on I simply felt no fear whatsoever, I just felt I had to get on and live every single day as it came, and not think of what was going to happen tomorrow.

■ ■ ■ ■ ■

In many cases, those chosen for work rather than the gas chambers did not yet know what had happened to the others. Some hoped that they had simply been taken to different barracks in another part of the camp. But those who had a chance to speak to other prisoners were soon told.

Barbara Stimler

Eventually they put us in fives and walk us into the shower room. By that time I already knew what was going on. I knew they were gassing people. I knew that the chimneys are burning the bodies. So when we got into the shower room, we looked at each other and we thought, 'God, is it gas or water?'

We're holding each other and praying to God what's going to come out, water or gas. So water came out, because I'm still here. If gas would come out I wouldn't be here.

Franz Brichta

On the first night it was pitch dark. I stood there and saw the licking flames out of the crematorium and said to myself, knowing by now what had happened, 'Which of these flames is my mother?'

Attached to each of the main gas chambers at Auschwitz were several huge ovens and a tall brick-built chimney. Each oven was capable of burning hundreds of bodies in a day. The SS forced some prisoners to work in the gas chambers themselves, carrying out bodies to be burned in the ovens.

Jewish women and children await their fate at Auschwitz

Some way of survival

Even among those people who survived the first selection on arrival at Auschwitz, most eventually died in the camp. They were either sent to the gas chambers later on, or died in the labour camp itself. Some were simply worked to death. Others died of disease, which was rife because of the filthy conditions. It was rare to survive in Auschwitz for more than three months. Nevertheless, for those who were fit and strong there was at least the possibility of remaining alive – and teenagers often had as good a chance as anyone. But survival depended on quick-thinking, willpower and luck.

Kitty Felix

I soon realized that there were people who were better dressed. They looked well-fed and I couldn't understand how it was that there were some that were on the point of death, which you saw all around the camp, and others were in a pretty good shape. And I realized that there's got to be some way of survival. At that point I didn't know the key to survival, but I did realize I was going to fight.

I realized that you have to learn the language. And it had its own expressions, the camp. One of the most important expressions was to 'organize', and to organize means to obtain, to buy, to sell, to get food. There was just one universal word for barter, and that was 'organize'. And if you lived by this principle, you learned how to get round certain situations. You had to organize your life and try and get into a better work party. The key to survival was a work party which enabled you to survive, because there were work parties where you couldn't survive and that became very apparent very soon. And you had to get away, that's another thing you had to learn: who were the people you had to get away from, people you should not associate with. There were all sorts of things you had to learn, and I'm afraid if you didn't learn all these things within the first few days, you were doomed.

Nothing was more disadvantageous than being on a work party actually working outside the camp, digging ditches, carrying stones, carrying cement. Any work party that worked outside was a disaster from the start because you were exposed to the elements, you were beaten, you had to walk to work in all conditions, in the rain and in the snow in the winter, in the heat of the summer. So if you could work within the camp compound or under cover somewhere inside, well, you were almost immediately at an advantage. If you could work, say, in a kitchen you were at a tremendous advantage, because you were working close to food. If you could work in the hospital compound, you were at an advantage.

The problem was, how did you manage to get into these work parties? There were people there working already, girls who were in the camp from the beginning. They were at an advantage, they survived the most horrendous times and of course they had the best occupations. And the newcomers were the most despised, because they didn't know their way around.

Well, you had to buy your way in, so you had to have something to give to somebody else, so that somebody else could do you a favour and perhaps help you to get into a better work party. The key to survival was instant adjustment, having a sixth sense of where danger came from, and perhaps even finding a way of being totally invisible, hiding behind the crowds, so that your face would never actually be known to anyone in charge, the people that were most feared.

Because some prisoners at Auschwitz were chosen to provide labour for its factories, there were more survivors from Auschwitz than from any of the other death camps. Of the hundreds of thousands of people sent to Treblinka, Belzec, Sobibor and Chelmno, only a tiny handful survived. But from Auschwitz, there were several thousand – many of them teenagers. Even so, they were only a tiny fraction of all those who had been sent there.

A huge pile of jumble

Not only did the Nazis use Auschwitz and other camps to murder millions of people, they also used them to steal every single item of value that they possibly could from their victims. Before they went into the gas chambers, people were ordered to hand over all their bags and suitcases. They were also told to undress and remove their watches and jewellery. Day by day, the Nazis collected vast amounts of these items and stored them near the gas chambers in a part of the camp nicknamed 'Kanada' (probably because Canada was commonly thought of as a 'land of plenty'). Other prisoners had to sort through these items so that anything valuable could be sent back to Germany or to German troops on the front line.

Auschwitz prisoners sorting bundles of clothing and other possessions

Kitty Felix

I didn't know what it was at the time, except I knew I was going to be sorting clothes. But what they were, where it was, we didn't know until we actually got there.

The nickname 'Kanada' I think originated from the SS who were in charge. Because it was known as the abundance of everything, there was just everything there. We marched out and we didn't know where we were going, in the direction of the crematoria, which of course I hadn't seen up till then. We did see the glow in the background, [but] the view was shielded by huge poplar trees. So we didn't quite know where we were being taken but we were taken in, in the direction of these poplars, and we passed lots and lots of fences and different camps which we didn't even know existed. We were taken to a very small area surrounded by a wood of birch trees.

The first thing that struck us [was] four tall chimneys and some low buildings. And a huge enormous pile of jumble, I can only describe it as jumble, which looked as though it was three or four storeys high. And in fact that pile of jumble were possessions of every description, open suitcases of photographs, clothes, shoes, everything mixed up, three storeys high.

We had a group of girls who would bring in piles of clothes and empty them at the end of the barrack and here again that built up to a huge pile as high as the ceiling. And it was sort of my job and the same with the group that I was working with – we all had to sort different clothes. Well at one point I had to sort men's jackets, so I had to go to this pile and look for nothing but men's jackets. I had to place these jackets on trestles, on a sort of table, and I had to feel all the seams for any hidden objects. And very often by the end of the day, or by the end of the shift – we had a 12-hour shift – we would collect a bucketful of jewellery, or bank notes or whatever was hidden in the jackets.

The Nazis even stole from the corpses of the people they had murdered. Before the bodies were burned in the ovens, the Nazis forced other prisoners to remove wedding rings from them and even to extract gold fillings from teeth.

■ ■ ■ ■ ■

'What shall I do? Where shall I be?'

After working all day, usually in conditions much more dangerous than those at the 'Kanada' block, prisoners would try to sleep for a few hours in overcrowded, lice-infested barracks. Twice a day, morning and evening, there was a roll call, when prisoners were inspected by the SS.

Armand Jakubovic, arrived in Auschwitz in 1944, aged 16

There were blocks of bunks three storeys high and varying from two to four people wide per storey. If you were unlucky, there were as many as 12 of you in one particular bunk. All these bunks were wooden, there wasn't anything by way of mattresses of course. You came into a routine of turning over in unison from one side to the other because I don't think it was wide enough for all of you to lie on your back without pushing into each other all the time.

Barbara Stimler

They used to wake us up at four o'clock in the morning. We had to stand outside in fives, counting us. You had to stay from five o'clock in the morning till ten o'clock sometimes, rain, snow, whatever.

Tauba Biber

We got up three o'clock in the morning. It was still dark and we waited and waited and they kept us sometimes for hours, till they counted us.

As far as they could, the Nazis made the prisoners run the camps on their behalf, just as they did in the ghettos. Certain prisoners – who became known as 'kapos' – were chosen to run each barrack (or block) and to carry out other tasks for the SS. These kapos were given certain privileges, and were less likely to be selected for the gas chambers, as long as they obeyed orders. But in obeying their orders, many kapos acted cruelly themselves. Not surprisingly, most ordinary prisoners came to fear and hate the kapos just as much as they did the SS guards.

Kitty Felix

The camp itself was run virtually by prisoners. Most of the time when you saw anyone of the SS hierarchy coming into the camp, you knew it didn't bode well, that something was going to happen, because they didn't come into the camp if there was no reason for it. They left the running of the camp to their own prisoner hierarchy that they had chosen. So if you saw anyone in a green [SS] uniform you immediately realized something was going to happen. And immediately your first thought was, 'What shall I do? Where shall I be? I must not be seen here. I must not be seen there. I've got to hide.' The worst was when the [SS] Kommandants came in. When they came in that definitely spelled disaster for the prisoners. It usually meant a selection for the [gas chambers].

Roman Halter

When you looked at an SS you knew that he wasn't with you. He wasn't for you. You could not pleadingly look in his face and say, 'Be kind to me, be compassionate, be loving.' This was not the person from whom you could demand that.

Kitty Felix

You soon realized that people who walked around the camp well-dressed, well-fed, usually with whips in their hands, were people that you had to avoid and they were part of the hierarchy. The camp hierarchy was a very complex structure and it was something that took some time to actually understand. You always had to avoid the kapos because they were only really carrying out the work of their superiors and so you knew you had to avoid them, and the best thing was to remain faceless and never really attract any attention whatsoever. Unless of course you had a friend who was a kapo, which was a very rare event if you were an ordinary prisoner.

Roman Halter

I knew that the roll call would be at six o'clock and I would wake up and wake other people up. Some were so afraid they will not wake up and be ready to get out because the kapos and the block people they used to come with sticks and beat people – *'Raus! Raus! Raus!'* – and you had to be out very quickly.

You simply thought of yourself

As each day dawned in Auschwitz, no prisoner knew if it would be their last. None knew what horrors awaited them. None knew if today would be the day that they would face their final 'selection', or the day that an SS guard would choose to punish them with a bullet. The only thing to do was to try to survive.

Kitty Felix

In my first 12 months in Auschwitz I could honestly say that I hadn't washed: I couldn't get access to water. It was the most incredibly difficult thing to do, because in charge of the water was again a particular privileged person, and unless you could give this person something you couldn't have access to water. So my skin became a mixture of red and grey. My friends de-loused me, and I de-loused them, but no way could we clean our skins of lice. So eventually we didn't worry about it. You tried to keep clean, very often you washed in your tea, because you couldn't drink it. Very often we washed in urine, it was considered a disinfectant. But of course it didn't actually make one clean.

I didn't actually worry too much about being dirty. My main concern was: find somewhere to sleep and find something to eat – and don't think about tomorrow. You just thought about this very one minute you were living, and nothing else. Nothing, nothing else.

Roman Halter

You simply thought of yourself, and when they said that you can sleep on that board, you just lay down and slept. And so you lived really for the hour, for the day. And you didn't know whether the selection would be the following day or whether you are going to be rounded up and taken to the gas chamber.

Kitty Felix

Your tattoo gave you a certain status. So if you had a huge number you were a new prisoner. But if you had a low number you were an old prisoner and so you no longer feared the hierarchy as you did when you were a newcomer.

Josef Perl

The chimneys were belching out fire and smoke, this went on day and night. Four thousand people a day were burnt. I always say: if the trees could only talk what horrific stories they would tell.

Although the full horror of the 'Final Solution' would not be revealed until after the War, the governments of Britain and the United States were almost certainly aware that people were being killed in large numbers at Auschwitz. Over the years there has been a lot of argument about whether they should have tried harder to bomb the camp or the railways leading to it. Until 1944 Allied planes could not reach Auschwitz because it was too far from their airbases. By June 1944, however, they had begun to close in on Germany and had established bases in Europe that brought the town within range. American bombers twice attacked Auschwitz's oil refineries and factories just a few miles away, but they did not target the camp itself, where the gas chambers continued to operate until November 1944.

Tauba Biber

There was a time we heard some aeroplanes, and we thought maybe they will bomb Auschwitz and our suffering will finish. We didn't think about the future. All we were hoping was that maybe it will come to an end.

Barbara Stimler

They were bombing, bombs came, I don't know if they were English or American. And we were praying to God they should bomb us together with the Germans, but it didn't happen.

On 7 October 1944 several hundred prisoners working in one of the gas chambers rebelled against their SS guards. Using explosives smuggled into the camp by Jewish women working in a nearby weapons factory, they blew up one of the gas chambers and escaped through the perimeter fence. But all of them were tracked down and killed. Similar revolts took place at Treblinka (2 August 1943), Sobibor (13 October 1943) and Chelmno (17 January 1945). All were savagely put down, and only a handful of prisoners escaped.

■ ■ ■ ■ ■

Britain and Germany 1942–1944

30 May 1942 The RAF launches its first 'thousand-bomber raid' against the German city of Cologne, which is severely damaged.

4 November 1942 In North Africa, the Germans are defeated at the Battle of Alamein – the first significant victory for the Allies.

2 February 1943 The German Sixth Army surrenders at Stalingrad, deep inside the Soviet Union. The Nazi advance eastwards is halted and the Russians gather strength for a counter-attack.

May 1943 Thanks to new technology and better tactics, the Allies are now winning the war at sea. After 40 German U-boats are sunk within a month, the Germans temporarily pull their U-boat fleet out of the Atlantic Ocean. They do return later in the War, but much-needed supplies are increasingly able to cross safely from the United States to Britain and the Soviet Union. Gradually the Allies begin to equip themselves to strike back at Hitler's armies in northern Europe.

Summer 1943 Together with American planes, now operating from British bases, the RAF intensifies its heavy bombing campaign against German cities. In a series of raids on Hamburg, a port in northern Germany, at least 20,000 people are killed and more than a million flee the city. The bombing campaign will continue until the very end of the War.

9 September 1943 Allied forces land at the southern tip of Italy and begin to fight their way northwards towards Germany. Italy soon surrenders, but Germany invades the northern part of Italy to prevent the Allies from making further progress.

January–April 1944 The Luftwaffe launches large-scale attacks on Britain for the first time since 1941. This period becomes known as the 'Little Blitz'.

May 1944 Allied forces mass in the south of England, in preparation for the invasion of Europe.

6 June 1944 – 'D-Day' After years of preparation, Allied armies finally launch their invasion of Europe from Britain. They land in northern France and fight their way towards Germany. A few weeks later, the Russians launch a massive offensive from the east. Germany is being attacked from two sides.

13 June 1944 The first V1 rocket, or 'flying bomb', lands in London. Hitler has launched his long awaited 'secret weapon'. The V2 will follow in September.

20 July 1944 Now convinced that Hitler is leading them towards disaster, a number of senior Nazi officers try to kill him with a bomb hidden in a briefcase. But Hitler survives and the plotters are executed.

August–September 1944 Most of France and Belgium are liberated by the Allies, who are gradually drawing near to Germany itself. Meanwhile the Russians are preparing for another huge advance from the east.

Losses on all fronts

Britain and Germany: 1943–1945

A big white arrow 218
Terrible things with carrots 221
We waited, glued to the radio 227
Something secret and new 230
'Christmas trees' 236

A big white arrow

In the early years of the War, many ordinary Germans had been delighted by the news of their victories in Europe.

Margarit Dierksen, Hanover, aged 13 in 1941

We had lessons in school, we had maps up, we were very patriotic and the War went Germany's way so of course it was very exciting, it was fantastic really. We won this battle and we won that battle and out came the flags. The English were the enemy and if Germany won a battle, that was fantastic and we were told about it at school and [we thought] 'Oh, good.' You never thought about it, you never thought about the families being left, the children who lost their parents. It was just Germany the winner and all this business.

By 1943, however, things had begun to change. Hitler's Propaganda Minister Josef Goebbels did his best to convince Germans that the War could still be won, but many of them had relatives who had been killed, wounded or captured on the Eastern Front and he did not try to hide the seriousness of the defeat at Stalingrad. In the meantime, Germany was coming under increasingly heavy attack from the air – something else that could scarcely be hidden from the general population.

Waltraudt Asser, Berlin, aged 16 in 1943

From 1943 onwards, which was when the bombing started in earnest I think the civilian population were demoralized. There were heavy losses on all fronts, particularly on the Russian front. Food was getting more and more scarce – rationing was becoming more and more severe. You were told as little as possible [about the War]. You were shown no foreign newspapers. It was illegal to listen to the foreign radio stations. You had to piece together whatever you could.

As Germans became increasingly concerned about the War, the Nazis became more determined than ever to prevent them having access to outside sources of news.

Anonymous girl, Stuttgart, aged 12 in 1943

We were constantly told to be watchful. We had been told about the brave little [Hitler Youth] who reported on his father for listening to a foreign station. And in the evening in bed I heard next door my uncle switching on [a foreign station]. And that was really terrible to me, because I felt I must report my uncle, and yet I couldn't, and was I a traitor?

Also, you were not supposed to be kind to any prisoners of war. You were supposed to hate these people, that was the most terrible thing. Where my grandmother lived, there was a factory opposite her house that was largely staffed by prisoners of war. In the evening you could hear them sing and you could see them walk about. There were French people there, and I found it very hard not to follow them round because I wanted to hear what they were saying, though I couldn't understand it. I liked the sound of the language.

Early in the war, Hitler had promised that he would raze British cities to the ground, but by 1943 it was German cities that were being destroyed in air raids that would continue until the end of the War. Most German families used public air-raid shelters, or else sheltered in their cellars.

Anonymous girl, Stuttgart

In our part, in the suburb, they dug [shelters] into the hillside and people dug in there and then you were allowed a seat if you had helped to dig. And there were men standing at the entrance who looked who was coming in. My mother didn't have to contribute because she had lots of children. It was a narrow passage with wooden seats both sides. It was very crowded. Water was constantly dripping in and you hung up little tin cans to catch the water. And you just sat in there, hoping for the best. If you wanted to go to the loo, you ran out to the nearest house and hoped you'd be all right.

People in Cologne, Germany, clearing up after an air raid

Jutta Zelle, from Siegen, aged 11 in 1943

Every family had one room designated in their house which was in the basement, which was reinforced with columns. We would put some cans down there and some drinking water and some blankets. And on the outside of the house was a big white arrow so that possible helpers, if the house had been completely damaged, would know where to dig.

My father owned a whole lot of books, and whenever he moved he packed his books into great big crates. My parents filled these boxes with books, put them in the basement in a square and we would huddle in between, the four of us, during a bombing attack.

> Like their British counterparts, some German children were evacuated from towns and cities. They either stayed with private families in the countryside, or went to stay in camps and hostels, usually run by their schools or by the Hitler Youth movement.

Waltraudt Asser

Most people were forced to go to their own cellars, which you might think were safe but if you were in them during a really hefty raid you wouldn't think so. We used to run to an official army bunker in Berlin. But it meant a terrifying dash and air raids came every night with dreadful regularity. I mean, the British, you could set your watch by them, the Americans during the day. The British did more concentrated bombing. I think it was just to terrorize the population, do as much damage as possible. Well, we hated anybody that was going to try and wipe us out.

> With the RAF flying at night, and the Americans carrying out daylight raids, by 1943 it was possible for the Allies to bomb Germany round the clock. Because the Americans flew in daylight, they usually aimed for specific military targets. On the other hand, the RAF carried out intensive 'carpet bombing' over a wide area, killing many more civilians.

Terrible things with carrots

In Britain, the worst of the mass air raids had finished in 1941, but there were many smaller-scale raids after that and it was impossible to predict when and where enemy planes would turn up next. 'Tip-and-run' raids became common, usually involving just a handful of bombers, or even a lone raider. London remained a prime target, but ports and coastal towns were also badly affected. (In the spring of 1942 Hitler ordered air raids on English towns known for their historic architecture, including Bath, York and Canterbury. These raids – which were a reprisal for British raids on historic German cities – became known as the 'Baedeker' raids, after a well-known series of tourist guidebooks.)

Increasingly, evacuees returned to their homes, though many stayed in the countryside until the end of the War. Wherever they were, children generally found they had more freedom than they were used to. Many fathers were away serving in the army, navy or air force, and because of the shortage of 'manpower' more and more mothers now had jobs.

Mother and daughter work together at a munitions factory in Sheffield

Joanna Rogers, Croydon, south London, aged 13 in 1943

Mother was working all day and Elizabeth and I had a great deal of freedom. We'd got bikes and we rode far and wide. We were six miles from Biggin Hill air[field]. We were given strict instructions as to what we could and couldn't do by mother each day, but she'd gone [to work] and we had freedom, you see. We used to just go and do other things. And we used to go out looking for crashed aircraft, anything we could find. Hopefully unexploded bombs.

Many women worked in 'war industries', making ammunition and other equipment. Others served in the forces, though not in combat roles. Most young men were 'called up' to the armed forces when they turned 18, and though there were plenty who dreaded that moment, some simply couldn't wait.

Stan Poole, decided to join the army in 1942, aged 16

As soon as I was 16, I went down to join up. I changed [my baptism certificate] from 1926 to 1924. We had the tip-off from our two mates that had done it. We wouldn't touch our birth certificate, we got our baptism certificate. That's not a legal document, so they can't do you for that.

Then I had to explain to my mother what I'd done. But she took it well. She didn't start bawling and howling, you know.

During the War there was a shortage of mineworkers in the coal industry, and in 1943 several thousand young men due for call-up to the armed forces were chosen by lottery and sent to work in coalmines instead.

By 1943, the War seemed to many children to have gone on for ever, and there seemed to be no end in sight. Some children had trouble remembering what life had been like before the War, and many had grown used to their fathers being away in the armed services.

Margaret Butler, Portsmouth

Once there was a knock at the door and I went. And there stood somebody in a uniform with a big beard. I went back into the lounge and I said to my mother, 'There's a man at the door wants to see you.'

So she put down her knitting, and she went to the door, and I heard her suddenly say, 'Tom!' And I went into the hall and there was my mother with her arms wrapped round this stranger.

He said, 'You don't even recognize me, do you?' And it was [my stepfather]. He'd been torpedoed three times, lost everything he had.

He'd lost about two stone in weight and of course had to grow his great big beard because he hadn't any shaving kit. And it was always his joke: 'Oh yes, you always looked after your mother and you wouldn't even let me in.'

Gradually, though, the War was beginning to turn in the Allies' favour, and as more and more U-boats were sunk, the Atlantic was becoming safer for shipping. Food parcels from America and parts of the British Empire had begun to arrive in 1941, and by 1943 more of them were getting through.

Joanna Rogers
Now these were a tremendous luxury because there were tins of fruit – and fruit we'd never even seen before, pawpaws and things like that. Which actually was a bit of a waste because we didn't really like them when they came. But they were exciting to open.

There were packets of dried egg that my sister and I got experts at making omelettes with. But the biggest thing of all was tins of Spam, which we felt were absolutely magnificent. To us it was the height of luxury.

Dried eggs came in the form of powder that had to be mixed with water. They were one of the first forms of 'processed food'. Advertised as 'The Miracle Meat', American-made 'Spam' was the world's first tinned meat that didn't need refrigerating. It began to arrive in Britain in 1941.

In the meantime the Government's 'Dig for Victory' campaign had proved highly successful. Gardens and public parks had been dug up all over Britain and flowerbeds turned into vegetable patches. Cartoon characters soon appeared in a poster campaign that encouraged people to use readily available vegetables like potatoes and carrots.

Joanna Rogers

We always had a lot of vegetables at home, because Daddy was a good gardener and ours was as good as anyone's. Mother went making terrible things with carrots in – like all mothers did. We used to have Christmas cake with carrot in and things like that. They were all pretty awful. We ate them, but they weren't particularly nice. The Ministry of [Food] used to do an awful thing about Doctor Carrot and Potato Pete and I think we used to think that was very silly.

At this stage my father kept rabbits. And it was a heartbreaking business when one of them had to be killed. But we did have rabbit-skin gloves and rabbit-skin hats. I don't think [we] were terribly keen on eating them, but we did.

I make a good Soup!

Says '**POTATO PETE**'

A poster featuring 'Potato Pete'

A popular slogan during the War was 'Make Do And Mend', and the 'Squander Bug' was another cartoon character intended to warn people about the dangers of wasting (or squandering) food and other supplies.

Joanna Rogers

We got short of things towards the end of the War, ever so many things. I mean mother and her metal curlers: she ran out of metal curlers and we had to use pipe cleaners to curl hair. Lots and lots of things we were short of. I mean we had saucepans that my father had had to mend because things like that you couldn't buy. And our wireless wasn't too good towards the end of the War – [Dad] was always tinkering with that. And of course it was very sad to see the car in the garage and not be able to use it [because of the petrol ration]. At school we did a great deal of collecting. There were lots of posters about squander bugs and things like that and we used to collect all used paper. We got completely into the habit of not wasting anything.

American GIs show English boys how to play baseball

To many people in Britain, who'd had to put up with years of rationing, the American servicemen who'd been steadily moving into the country since

1942 seemed very well off. GIs – so-called because of the initials stamped on their uniforms – brought plentiful supplies of cigarettes, sweets and other luxury goods that were hard to come by in Britain. They also brought the latest American fashions in jazz music and dance. All this tended to make them popular with children and teenage girls – but unpopular with parents.

Margaret Butler

We had a lot of troops stationed around the area. Of course, my parents [said], 'You don't talk to American soldiers.' Well, of course my *friends* talked to American soldiers and they went to dances. So I thought, 'Well, what they can do I can do.'

And they came to me one day and said, 'Look, there's a big concert at the Americans' camp tonight. Do you want to come?' And I said, 'Yes, but please don't tell my mum.' So I went and when we got to the camp this American said, 'Well, look, sneak around the back.' And that was the night that Glenn Miller came and played.

 Glenn Miller (1904–1944) was a popular swing bandleader of the wartime era. One of his most famous tunes was the 'Chattanooga Choo Choo'.

We waited, glued to the radio

By the spring of 1944, everybody was expecting an Allied invasion of Europe that would at last challenge Hitler's hold on the continent. The south-east of England was bursting with troops – mostly British, American, and Canadian, but also including many Poles, Frenchmen and Czechs. As preparations were made to transport an enormous army across the Channel, roads, airfields and ports were busier than they'd ever been during the War. The time and location of the final attack were top secret, but it was impossible to disguise its scale.

Margaret Butler

I remember seeing boats suddenly appearing in the harbour, lots and lots of boats. Between Langston Harbour and Hayling Island there's quite a big stretch of water. And you suddenly saw these boats and you realized that if you stepped on to a boat here you could probably have walked on each boat right across to Hayling Island.

Joanna Rogers

There were lots and lots of convoys. Tanks, guns, all camouflaged with greenery and netting, and obviously the invasion was coming. There was stuff everywhere, everywhere was military. Every lane had something moving down it – convoys, tanks on low-level loaders. And we used to see gliders. And obviously something was on.

American military vehicles parked on a Southampton street on the day before D-Day

Dennis Hayden, evacuee in Newbury, Berkshire, aged 12

To go to school we had to go past Greenham Common, which was a big United States Air Force base. And of course we could look through the fence, across the runways, and see all the various planes landing and taking off. Then we suddenly noticed a lot of aeroplanes beginning to form up. Then gliders appearing and ropes all coiled up and a lot more equipment coming.

Ronald McGill, Vauxhall, aged 14

We used to go down camping in Surrey. And one day we were pulling a trek-cart and there was a long, leafy road and there was all these tanks there and Canadians. And we got to chat to them, and spent the whole day with [them] and they made a fuss of us children: gum and sweets. They wouldn't tell us what they were doing or anything, but we were taken on the tank. I'll never forget that day. And within two weeks of that it was D-Day and that's where they were going.

Joanna Rogers

The early part of [June] my father knew it was on, and he told us, and everybody around us knew. And we waited, glued to the radio.

Dennis Hayden

One particular night coming home there seemed to be [a] great deal more activity, [a] lot of lorries. Soldiers and people getting on and off these aircraft, equipment being put on. There was a lot of noise during the night [and] the next morning [when we] went to school, the aerodrome was completely deserted. There wasn't a thing left. There was no aircraft, no gliders, no troops, no trucks, just the odd guard walking around. And when we went to school we were told by the teachers that D-Day had started.

Margaret Butler

On the day before D-Day I'd taken the dog for a walk and the soldiers were sitting outside tents. And one fellow came over, he said to me, 'Can you post a letter for me? We're not allowed out of here and I would like my wife to get this letter.'

And I thought, 'Supposing he's a spy and he's telling the Germans where he's stationed. We shall have bombs here.' Then I thought, 'No, maybe he's not, maybe he's all right.' So I did take the letter and I posted it.

Well, the next morning when I took the dog for a walk there was not a soldier to be seen.

Joanna Rogers

Then the day of the invasion we were thrilled, thrilled to the core. You know, we thought: this was it. It was going to be the end.

The D-Day landings began at dawn on 6 June 1944, when Allied troops began wading ashore from landing craft along six beaches on the northern French coast in Normandy. Around 185,000 men were landed in what was the largest seaborne invasion in history. Inland, other troops were dropped by parachute or came in on gliders.

Something secret and new

At the end of January 1944, British people had again heard the throb of massed planes in the sky. This 'Little Blitz', as it became known, had continued until April but then petered out. By D-Day, it seemed that the Luftwaffe *had done its worst, but the Germans had now developed some new weapons, and the first of them arrived in Britain less than a week after the Allied landings in France.*

Joanna Rogers

[One morning] we heard this funny noise like a motorbike and we saw this little plane coming and I thought it had got a funny engine. It was coming low and it had got flames coming out of its tail.

We were standing by our front door and Elizabeth said to me, 'It's coming down!' Of course we didn't rush in, we rushed out, and it landed about a mile up the road and we said, 'It's exploded.' But we thought it was a plane. It had got funny chopped off wings and it was making a funny little *putt putt* noise like a motorbike.

Daddy came home from work late and said it was something secret and new. And we were a bit frightened.

Churchill had warned people that Britain might come under 'new forms of attack' as the War neared its end. And now Hitler had launched his new 'Vengeance Weapons' (V1s) – the world's first guided missiles. These 'robot bombs' or 'pilotless planes' could strike Britain without the need for German aircrew, which were now in short supply.

Derek Milton, Kennington, south London, aged 15

I remember the first night they were used, and there was this air raid on at night. And I [was] looking out as usual, and I said, 'Look, they got one, it's on fire.' Of course – I didn't know – it was a V1. And you got the flames coming out from the rocket motor. And [I said], 'Oh, the anti-aircraft, it's unusual for them to hit anything.' Of course in the morning I read the papers and I knew what it was all about.

On the first night, 12–13 June, Hitler sent only a handful of V1s, but soon they were coming day and night in a steady procession, with up to 100 arriving each day. They fell all over south-east England, with about half of them reaching London. The worst-affected area, between the Kent coast and London, soon became known as 'Bomb Alley'.

Edward Butt, returned evacuee to West Ham, east London, aged 14

V1s were whizzing over like nobody's business, and I thought, 'Well, thanks very much, Hitler, it's a nice welcome.' Life just stopped during [the] attacks. The radio was turned off and you just sat quiet and listened and listened for the beat of the 'doodlebug'. And as soon as that beat stopped – under the table, quick!

A V1 flying bomb

Because of the noise they made, people in Britain called V1s 'buzz bombs' or 'doodlebugs'. They were 8 metres long and weighed 2.5 tons. With a range of about 150 miles, they were launched from long ramps, built mainly near the northern French coast. Their engines were designed to cut out once they were over the target area.

Sylvia Bell, Surbiton in Surrey, aged 9

You knew that as long as the flames were coming out at the back and the engine was going you were OK. And you just looked, waiting for the engine to stop because then you knew it was coming down.

Although Londoners had grown used to bombing, there was something particularly frightening about these new weapons. Not surprisingly, more than a million people decided to move out of London once again.

Joanna Rogers, re-evacuated with her family to Buckinghamshire

[It] was a hairy journey because they were coming down all the time. And we were sitting in the train on the line up to Charing Cross and we saw people standing outside their shelters pointing, and suddenly we saw them all dive in. We were on the train and we couldn't do anything about it. Well, the front of the train was hit. It wasn't derailed but it was hit and the driver was killed. And all the windows were broken but we were on the floor so we weren't hurt, we just had glass round us.

Ronald McGill, with his mother, visiting an aunt in Clapham, south London

[As] we got off the bus, the sirens sounded. And we were walking along and we heard the flying bomb coming. Well, we looked back and it was coming out of the cloud, low clouds, and the engine stopped. We were about 60 yards from my aunt's outside shelter in the street.

Well, we ran, we really did run, and we fell into the door of the shelter as the flying bomb hit the house behind. And both houses collapsed, and all you saw was just choking blackness, and we heard the house roar [and] come down. Then breaking glass.

And when we came out, all we had left was half of the front of my aunt's house. [She'd been] in the front room waving to us, and it saved her life, because the wardens ran up and managed to get her out. But people were buried in the house behind her and some were killed.

That was the last straw. We left for Blackpool the following morning. My mother said, 'Our luck can't keep up, it nearly ran out then.'

V Nearly 10,000 V1 rockets were launched at Britain, though many were shot down by anti-aircraft guns or fighter planes. Still, more than 2,500 rockets fell on London.

A small girl is rescued from a house where a V1 bomb crashed

By the end of August, Allied troops in France had overrun the main V1 launching sites, and many people who had left London began returning to their homes again. However, the Germans soon had a more destructive rocket that could be fired from further away and was capable of destroying an entire street, not just the odd house.

Ronald McGill

One day we were playing cricket on Barnes Common when a V2 – the first one ever – came down, and we were within a mile of there. When I went back to Dad that evening I said, 'That was a German thing, that noise.' And he said, 'No it wasn't, it was probably a gas thing blew up.' I said, 'No, there was too many soldiers and police. It's something to do with Germany.' He wouldn't believe me, but afterwards [we heard] it was the first V2 rocket.

 So destructive were these new weapons that at first the British Government tried to deny that they existed, claiming that the explosions were caused by accidents at gas mains. This led some people to nickname V2s 'flying gas mains'.

Edward Butt

What I wasn't ready for, and neither was anybody else, was the V2s. And I can remember the Sunday morning a V2 dropped. 'What was that?' Bang! And then there was this almighty explosion. And because they went faster than sound, after the explosion came the sound of the rocket coming through the air. It was eerie.

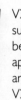 V2s were 14 metres long and weighed 12 tons. They were supersonic rockets, which meant they arrived several seconds before the sound waves that carried the noise of their approach. As a result, it was impossible to hear one coming and they could not be shot down. All together, about 1,000 V2s landed in Britain, killing around 3,000 people.

After the War, Hitler's chief V2 rocket scientist Wernher von Braun helped the United States Government develop its own rocket programme – including the space rocket that landed the first men on the moon in 1969.

Sylvia Limburg, central London, aged 9

It was a time when you didn't really have any warning of some kind of disaster. It just fell out of the sky and took everyone by surprise.

V2s weren't the only form of disaster likely to strike households in Britain and in many cases, especially after D-Day, it didn't fall from the sky – it simply knocked at the door.

235

Ronald McGill, working as a telegram boy in west London

The flying bombs were still coming around so we used to ride round with tin hats on. That's when I really grew up, very quickly, because we were delivering all the death telegrams [informing people that a relative had been killed in action]. And we were told that when we took the telegrams we were to try and knock on either side to try and get somebody to come in with you. The person shouldn't be left alone.

One I had to go to was near Hammersmith Bridge. And the lady, she must have realized I was knocking on either side and she came out and she said, 'That's for me, isn't it?' And she just fainted, fell down on the floor.

She hadn't even opened it. And I managed to get another neighbour [to] pull her in, and they opened it and it was her husband and he'd been killed. And, you know, I just stood there, I didn't know what to do. It's a terrible thing.

I remember once when I went round the block four times before I stopped. You know, it was giving them a little bit longer. But they always knew. As soon as they saw your uniform they just knew.

'Christmas trees'

In Germany, the Nazis tried to play down the significance of the successful D-Day landings, but to some people it was clear that the War was now being lost.

Anonymous girl, Stuttgart, aged 13

In the school suddenly we were told, *'Sie kommen!'* – 'They're coming!' And we imagined them coming straight away and one of our teachers gave a very patriotic speech, saying [that] now every man, woman and child must be prepared to defend us. We were all crying and wanted to go home. The other teacher just sat there and cried with us. And that sort of made it all very imminent, very terrifying.

In fact it would take several months for the Allies to advance as far as Germany itself. In the meantime, they launched more air raids – raids that were far heavier and more sustained than those of the Blitz in Britain.

Jutta Zelle

I had a good singing voice. So they had put me into a [Hitler Youth] group and we were singing at a wedding at a hotel and we did not hear the alarm. The staff in the hotel forgot about us in the backroom [where] we were practising. So we were singing our hearts out and we had the lights on, it was a dark December day. And suddenly the lights went out and the bombing started. We scattered every which way – our instinct was to get outside. The main door was burning, everything was already burning.

Anonymous girl, Stuttgart

There was an air raid without any warning and my father made us all run to the shelter, which was in the hillside. And we ran out and the 'Christmas trees' were coming down, lighting up everything and the bombs were just falling like mad and I was lying in the gutter. I had had an operation just before on my tonsils and it all started bleeding so I was a real mess.

I thought I'd lost my brother, although he was already in the shelter but I didn't know. And I remember coming home and there was just fire and damage everywhere. That was pretty foul.

 'Christmas trees' was the nickname Germans gave to the marker flares dropped by RAF reconnaissance planes just before a raid. The flares would light up the area to make it an easier target for the bombers.

Jutta Zelle

I somehow got up the steps, and I was standing in the frame of a second-storey window. Everything was burning around me, and I knew I had to jump, but around the hotel was a wrought iron fence. And I suddenly saw a Russian prisoner of war, standing down behind this fence. (Next to this hotel there were some barracks and we knew their uniforms. But those places had already been bombed too so they were all scattering around.) And he waved and gestured and I realized he wanted me to jump. Well I did jump, and he broke my fall. And he just grabbed me by the hand and we had to jump over burning trees, and we ran and ran and ran.

The city was completely destroyed. It was an old, old city. About 800 years old. The entire old city was destroyed and on fire.

[I] did manage to get home, only to find that my father had gone out to look for me. He had made his way down to the hotel and he found my sweater in a big heap of rubble. He came home hours later, and I was standing by an open window in the house, and I saw this old, old man coming down the street and I realized it was my father, and I called to him and he thought he had lost his mind when he saw me because he had just fished this rag of a sweater out of the rubble. So that was a very emotional day.

Anonymous girl, Stuttgart

It depended very much on how conscious you were of what was going on. My little sister who was born [in] 1940 didn't seem to suffer at all. In fact Christmas 1944 we had at least four or five air raids and each time we came back [from the shelter] we had to light the candles that we had. And next morning she was radiantly happy and said, 'Oh, what a nice Christmas we've had. We could light the candles five times!'

■ ■ ■ ■ ■

The ruins of Cologne in 1945 after Allied bombing

For most children, as Germany became increasingly penned in by the Allied armies approaching from both sides, daily life became more and more difficult. Shortages of food, clothes and other essential supplies became increasingly severe and rationing was strict.

Margarit Dierksen, Celle, aged 17 in 1944

I remember I desperately wanted a new pullover to go to school with. So the shop in the village – the lady in there, she said, 'I've got a lot of sugar bags' – sugar came in great big bags – 'If you want, [you can] take these sugar bags home and unpick them and pull all these threads out.' I knitted myself a jumper with that, and then somebody else gave me a couple of waterproof gas-mask bags and I made myself an anorak thing, and I went to school [in it].

I used to walk two miles to the nearest station and it was winter then and very cold. And we used to catch the train, and there was a whole gang of us. We were only allowed to go in the last compartment because I suppose we were a bit noisy. But it was such a cold day that we disobeyed and we went in the first carriage behind the engine. And we got attacked by a low-flying aeroplane. He attacked the engine and of course hit the first compartment. Had we stayed in the last compartment, we would have got away with it. But I lost a friend, she was killed sitting opposite me. Anyway, the train stopped and everybody got out [and] ran across a field, which was white with snow, to get away from the train in case it blew up.

And before the Christmas holidays at school, we were all called into assembly and we were told that we could sit an emergency exam because the war was getting so close that we didn't have to come back. You see, I was going to leave in a year's time anyway at 18, and we were told that we didn't have to come back, we could sit our exams and that would be the end for us. Because of the war coming so close, everything during those days was gradually closing down.

■ ■ ■ ■ ■

Germany 1945

January 1945 As the Allies close in on Germany, Hitler has now lost most of the territory he had conquered in the early years of the War. In Poland, the Nazis have already abandoned Auschwitz after attempting to destroy its gas chambers with explosives. They have forced many surviving prisoners to march to concentration camps in Germany. By the end of the month, Soviet forces reach Auschwitz and liberate the remaining survivors. They have already begun to cross the eastern borders of Germany itself, causing many thousands of German civilians to flee westwards. It is now increasingly obvious that Germany is going to lose the War, but Hitler orders his armies to fight on.

13 February 1945 While Allied armies approach the River Rhine in western Germany, British and American planes target the medieval German city of Dresden in one of the most destructive air raids of the War. The city, which is crowded with refugees from the east, is almost completely destroyed. At least 35,000 people are killed.

April 1945 As they overrun more German territory, British and American soldiers liberate several concentration camps, including Dachau and Belsen. Inside they find thousands of prisoners dead or dying from starvation and disease.

25 April 1945 On the River Elbe, in central Germany, American soldiers advancing from the west meet Soviet soldiers fighting from the east. The Allies have linked up at last, cutting Germany in two. Hitler orders Germans to fight on.

30 April 1945 Surrounded by Soviet soldiers, who are now fighting their way into Berlin street by street, Adolf Hitler shoots himself in his underground bunker. Two days later Berlin finally falls to the Soviet army.

7 May 1945 Admiral Doenitz, now in charge of Germany, authorizes the unconditional surrender of the German army to General Eisenhower, Supreme Commander of the Allied Forces. The War in Europe is over.

8 May 1945 In Britain, huge crowds celebrate Victory in Europe (VE) Day. The War continues in the Pacific, however, where Germany's ally Japan refuses to surrender. Meanwhile Germany is divided into four zones, each occupied by one of the principal Allies: Britain, France, the Soviet Union and the United States.

6 and 9 August 1945 The United States drops its newly developed atomic bombs on the Japanese cities of Hiroshima and Nagasaki. These bombs immediately kill around 150,000 civilians, though many more die later from the effects of radiation.

14 August 1945 Japan declares a ceasefire and formally surrenders two weeks later, bringing an end to the Second World War.

November 1945 In the German city of Nuremberg, where the Nazis held their annual rallies, the Allies put 22 leading Nazis on trial for war crimes.

Ruins

Germany: 1945

The Russians were so close   244
'Dresden is burning'   247
'Don't shoot us!'   250
She could hardly speak   255
Salmon and shrimp paste   258
Nothing to eat   259

The Russians were so close

By the beginning of 1945, a force of more than two million Soviet troops was pressing towards Germany's eastern borders, while British and American forces moved in from the other side. Hitler's armies were losing ground on all fronts, and as more and more German soldiers were captured or killed, the Nazis turned increasingly to teenagers to fill their ranks.

Jutta Zelle, Siegen, aged 13

Klaus, my brother, was by that time 15 [or] 16, and he really could not be out in the open because the boys were taken right off the street. It happened to a young friend of ours, who was my brother's age, who was walking home and suddenly two SS men were walking right and left of him. And they were just simply going to grab him right off the street and send him to the front.

In a flash, the street car came by and in a split second he jumped on, jumped out on the other side, and then disappeared. Those moments came for many young people. Your life depended on an instant reaction.

■ ■ ■ ■ ■

Meanwhile, hundreds of thousands of German civilians from the eastern parts of Germany were fleeing westwards. This was partly to avoid the vicious fighting that was sure to come as Hitler ordered his remaining armies to turn eastern German cities into defensive 'fortresses'. It was also to avoid occupation by the Soviets, who were greatly feared by the German population because of their reputation for brutality towards civilians.

Edith Warthold, living in a village near Breslau, a 'fortress' town in eastern Germany, aged 13

In 1945 everybody had to be evacuated – mainly women and children because there were hardly any men around. In our school camp, we were told we have to move. So one day a lorry arrived and our teacher said, 'Now pack all your things, girls. We will have to leave this little village.' And children were sent further away into the middle of Germany, for security. We did not know as children that the Russians were so close, because our teachers would not tell us these things.

German refugees in 1945

Margarit Dierksen, living on a farm in Celle, near Hanover, central Germany, aged 18

We were in this farmyard, my mother, my grandmother and myself one day, and all of a sudden we heard a rumble coming down the road and my mother said, 'What on earth is that?' And it was a covered wagon, like a cowboy wagon. There was an old granny, a horse which was on its last legs and a younger woman, and it came past our farm and the farmer's wife came out and she said, 'Oh, more refugees.' And when they opened the flap at the back of this wagon, it was full of pillows and full of feather beds, and five kids came out. And this family, when the Russians came, they fled. The father was in the army and there was this poor woman, this poor mother with this old lady. She'd collected her children and put them all in this wagon and walked right up to where we were. It's hundreds of miles but they walked and walked and walked. To get away from there. They were afraid of the Russians coming.

> On 30 January 1945, thousands of German refugees fleeing from the Russians crammed aboard the *Wilhelm Gustloff*, flagship of the Nazis' 'Strength Through Joy' cruise liners. It was designed to carry 2,000 passengers, but there were three to five times that number aboard that night. The ship was torpedoed by a Russian submarine in the Baltic Sea and as many as 9,000 people are thought to have lost their lives. It was the worst maritime disaster in history.

Refugees were not the only people on the move. As the retreating Nazis vacated many of the concentration camps and slave labour camps that they'd built, they moved their occupants to other camps deeper inside Germany. Some were forced to march hundreds of miles in the depths of winter, and many died on the way.

Ryvka Berkowicz, transported from slave labour in Hamburg to Belsen, 1945, aged 16

After a couple of days the train stopped and they were shouting and screaming, 'Come on, come on, get off the train', and we jumped off the train and we were lined up in fives and were taken on a long road marching. The whole journey, from there to the camp, was littered with dead bodies. That's when I got really frightened. I was without my mother, I was still only a child and I was so scared and I wanted to cry but I was too scared to cry. I was too scared to do anything.

'Dresden is burning'

On 13 February 1945 the historic German city of Dresden, where half a million people lived, was overcrowded with tens of thousands of German refugees from the east. Famous mainly for its medieval architecture and beautiful porcelain, Dresden was not an industrial city and had never been heavily bombed. (Locals used to joke that Churchill had a favourite aunt living there, who kept them safe from attack.) But that evening the Allies chose Dresden as the target of one of their heaviest air raids.

Ruined buildings after the bombing of Dresden

Edith Warthold, passing through Dresden after being evacuated from Breslau, aged 13

After various days of travelling we arrived in Dresden. I remember we were there on a Sunday and our teacher said, 'Well, maybe tomorrow morning we will get another train and we will go off to a proper school camp and we all will be together and we will be safe.'

Monday morning we had to pack all our small belongings, our school satchel, we had to take all that along. And we went to the main station in Dresden, and we had to wait a very long time. It was very cold, it was February and it was bitterly cold. There were a great number of people at the station, mainly refugees from the east, mainly women, very few men. And it was pandemonium all round and our teacher tried to keep us together. As girls we were about 20 or 25 [in number] and she was responsible for us.

Suddenly sirens started wailing and we had to run downstairs to the bunker underneath the station. And there were many people, a few thousand, it was a huge bunker. Then we settled there and it took till about eight or nine o'clock and then the first bombing started. And we could hear the bombs outside. And we could feel the detonations.

Later some people went outside to see what happened. And they would say, 'Oh dear, Dresden is burning. Dresden is burning. It looks terrible, there is fire everywhere.'

Then later the alarms went off again and the second raid started, which was really the worst part of it. It never stopped for a very long time and our bunker started to disintegrate. Everybody was terribly scared and people started shouting and women were crying. Some people would shout, 'We're drowning! We're drowning!' because there were burst water pipes at the back of the bunker. Because the water level started to rise.

So we were trapped there. And it went on and on and the bombing didn't stop for a long time.

> The bombing of Dresden was so severe that it caused a 'firestorm' above the city. This happens when hundreds of separate fires caused by incendiaries join together and form one single conflagration. This sucks in air from the surrounding area, causing winds like tornadoes. Temperatures under and around the storm become so great that anything capable of catching fire – including buildings and people – bursts into flames.

Then much later, it must have been three or four o'clock in the morning, it suddenly was quiet again and people were hysterical. There were clouds of smoke in the bunker. One couldn't really see anything [but] we saw our teacher – she was a very tall lady and she had a great big fur coat, and we recognized her and we started all getting towards her. People were walking all over us and between us, and if you were in the way they would just pull you down and trample on top of you. And it was really terrible. And people started crying and some were injured, not by the bombing, but by being kicked or whatever. And then the smoke got thicker and thicker and somebody said, 'We have to do something. We have to get out. We have to get out.' And we all shouted together: '*Hilfe!* [Help!] … *Hilfe!* … *Hilfe!*'

Nothing happened. Nobody could reach us, I suppose, and we were stuck. And I was very, very scared. We all started crying, and I prayed, 'Oh dear God, please let me see my mother again.'

Some time went past, and later somebody broke through the wall at the far end and we could feel fresh air coming through. And everybody suddenly moved towards that hole and said, 'We have to get through there.' And somebody said, 'No we can't because there are flames.' I was terrified and I held on to my friend Renata and we said, 'No, we wait here till we really have to go.' And then another exit suddenly appeared, and it seemed that people from the outside had broken through different walls to rescue us.

When we got out we didn't recognize anything because it was all in ruins, and there were flames and there were injured people and people were crying and women were shouting for their children. Nobody knew where everybody was. And we sat in a little heap and then our teacher appeared from somewhere, she saw us.

Later we had to climb on to lorries, and everything was still burning. And we travelled away from Dresden to some school and the Red Cross sisters made us lie down and they gave us something to eat and drink. Then [a few days later] my teacher called me and said, 'There's somebody who would like to see you.' And I went upstairs and there was my mother. [She] had returned to find me because she heard of the bombing in Dresden and she did not know where I might be. By then we were only six girls left from our class. We don't know where the others disappeared to – we didn't hear of them anymore.

■ ■ ■ ■ ■

'Don't shoot us!'

During the spring of 1945, with Hitler still refusing to surrender, Allied soldiers gradually fought their way deep into Germany. In the west, British, French and American troops began to capture important German towns. From the east, the Soviets headed towards Berlin. As battles raged all around them, it was a dangerous and uncertain time for German civilians. Many simply hid in their cellars and hoped the fighting would be over quickly.

Anonymous girl, Stuttgart

I was terrified of whatever the outcome would be, because I didn't want us to win, which means Germany. And I had no idea what it was going to be like if the others won. But I was very soon persuaded that the Germans were going to lose.

Margarit Dierksen

Everything during those days was gradually closing down. The British troops gradually came nearer and nearer and then the shelling started. There was gunfire from one side, from the Germans, and gunfire from the other side, from the British, and it came over our village.

Jutta Zelle

In March or early April we had the front in our little town for over ten days. One day German soldiers were lying in the trenches. The next day American soldiers were lying in the trenches when we peeked out. And the soldiers were shooting back and forth.

Anonymous girl, Stuttgart, aged 14

The Americans were in the north and the French were in the south. We didn't know who was going to conquer us. And that day we sat in the shelter and I was pretty hungry and we had our rations allocated to each child – every week so much bread – and you kept it in a tin box and tried to hide it from everybody else, and also from the rats because we had lots of rats by that time.

I remember being hungry and wanting to go home and get my bread so I told my mother I wanted to go and spend a penny. And instead I ran home, going downhill and crossing over a main road into Stuttgart. When I got towards it I heard a lot of firing and I stopped short and a tank came. It was the first black man of my life. It was a very, very black soldier in there. He trained his machine guns right on me and I just froze and looked at him. I was so surprised that he was so black. And he just looked at me. And then after a bit he swung the turret round and drove on.

And coming back, the tanks came at a distance of 100 metres or something like that and I waited for a gap, and then I dashed back into the shelter and I said to them, 'They're black!'

Some soldiers from French colonies in North Africa fought for the Allies. There were also many black soldiers in the US army. Many Germans had only come across black people in Nazi propaganda, which portrayed them as racially inferior.

Hannah Voss, Hamburg, aged 17

For days we'd heard the rumblings in the distance and it came closer and closer and the raids were increasing. Mother felt very insecure. Our garden backed east, and that's where they started from, the bombardment, artillery. We just sat in this fortified basement, really, and *bang, bang, bang, bang.*

There was a bit of a lull. And something had fallen in the garden. Splinters and shrapnel were all about. The top of the chimney had been shot down, with a terrific clatter, and the roof had virtually gone. I looked out, and there was a tank going along at the back. And we thought, 'Oh well, this is it, it's finished.' But we didn't dare come out because they might take a pot shot.

And then we just sat tight, talking amongst ourselves. And then we heard footsteps above. And we thought, 'Ah well, what's this? Are they rifling the place? Or are they soldiers or what?' So we thought we'd better let them know we're here, in case they set the place on fire.

So we thought it was a good idea to just knock on the ceiling. Which is what we did. We all stood here. And he came down with his gun at the ready. And all I can remember saying is, 'Oh you lovely man, don't shoot us!'

In April 1945 came the battle for the German capital of Berlin, which was surrounded by Soviet troops. Hitler had holed himself up in a huge bunker under the Chancellery, one of the main government buildings. From there he ordered what was left of his desperately ragged armies to defend what was left of the city. They were to fight on 'to the last man and the last shot'.

Soviet soldiers enter Berlin

Waltraudt Asser, Berlin, aged 18

Once I realized that losing the War was inevitable I was just hoping it would be quick and I would survive it. The Russians were already pounding us with their artillery [and] the curiously lumbering, slow planes they had.

It was on my birthday actually that things were coming to a head. Where before we'd heard the rumours of fighting in certain outlying districts, we were beginning to hear it. We also heard of street fights, actual streets being fought over that we knew by name that were near enough to make us realize that it was only a question of time. And we were told that some SS snipers had dug themselves in, [not] that far from where we lived. And there was terrible fighting going on.

We felt [the Nazis] should have surrendered, but we knew that they wouldn't because they'd already announced that. They tried to turn people into soldiers that weren't soldiers and in many cases they couldn't even give them any weapons. The old Home Guard, some over 70, they gave them, I think they were Belgian rifles with no ammunition. And they expected them to go out and fight. The children, they were issued with *Panzerfaust* – and that is a terrible weapon.

In September 1944 Hitler had ordered the formation of a Home Guard (or *Volkssturm*) as a last line of defence for Germany. All male civilians aged 16–65 were ordered to join, but in practice the *Volkssturm* mainly consisted of elderly men and teenagers because most other men had already been called up. The *Panzerfaust* was an anti-tank rocket launcher. During the fight for Berlin, units of Hitler Youth boys, some of them as young as 14, were given these weapons and ordered into battle on bicycles.

In one of the last-known photographs of Hitler, he awards a medal to a 12-year-old Hitler Youth soldier

Eventually, with his Berlin bunker surrounded by Soviet soldiers, Hitler finally realized it was all over and shot himself to avoid capture. Through the chaos of Berlin, rumours of his death quickly began to circulate.

Waltraudt Asser

We couldn't quite believe it actually. We'd thought that it was entirely possible that he would pop up somewhere else.

But within days of Hitler's death German generals surrendered and the War in Europe was over.

Margarit Dierksen

Well, we were just glad the War was over, we really were. There was a curfew at night – we weren't allowed out after dark – but otherwise it was as if a great weight fell off our shoulders because there was no shooting, no air raids, nothing. Everybody just thought, 'Well we'll have to get on with it now and pick up our life.'

■ ■ ■ ■ ■

She could hardly speak

As Allied armies overran Germany they were horrified by what they found inside the Nazi concentration camps, which were ravaged by disease and full of starving prisoners wandering among piles of unburied bodies. Many prisoners were so ill that the Allies could do nothing to help them, and thousands died even after the camps were liberated.

Berek Obuchowski, from Poland, Theresienstadt concentration camp, Czechoslovakia, aged 17

I had just got over typhoid, this was my second typhoid – stomach typhoid. I was very weak and I also had problems with my [broken] foot. It didn't heal up properly, so I wasn't in a good condition. But nevertheless, when I looked around me, I didn't complain too much.

Jack Aizenberg, from Poland, Theresienstadt concentration camp, aged 17

The bad thing about Theresienstadt where I'm concerned was the starvation. On the liberation day I was more dead than alive. I think that in another day I would have been dead. I had this feeling of floating. I did not care whether I lived or not.

Klara Hochhauser, from Hungary, Mauthausen concentration camp, Austria, aged 13

There were these American soldiers, they had no food on them, they just found us accidentally. They were just driving past and saw these people sitting through the gate. As they had nothing on them they didn't know what to do. The only thing they had on them was cigarettes and they gave us all a cigarette. And we all tried to eat it.

Former prisoners at Belsen concentration camp after liberation

Some German civilians knew next to nothing about the conditions inside the concentration camps, though most had probably glimpsed enough to know that they were terrible places. Perhaps only a few knew the whole truth, and so the opening up of the camps after the War was a shock for many German people too.

Hannah Voss

I had heard of concentration camps, but neither my mother nor anybody acquainted with us knew of Bergen-Belsen, which from our town must be within half an hour, 40 minutes, in the car. And during all our roamings and ramblings and cycling in the area, we just never knew.

[After the War] the local population was made aware of [it] officially. And people denied it. They said, 'No, no, Germany didn't do this.' Because that was the first many people actually heard of concentration camps.

And they said, 'No, this isn't true. And certainly not in our area. Oh no, no, no.' So my mother approached the British man, Major Somebody-or-other, who was in charge of the town, and said she would be willing to actually go to Belsen and bring back her impressions to pass on to other people.

And she came back looking horror-stricken. And she could hardly speak because of what she'd seen. And she duly wrote down her report and tried to pass it on to others. But nobody was interested really.

After the War the Allies forced many German civilians to visit the concentration camps, or to go and watch films made by the troops who had liberated the camps, showing what they had discovered. They wanted people to see what 12 years of Nazi rule had led to.

Salmon and shrimp paste

In Britain, the German surrender was greeted with jubilation and the following two days were declared national holidays. The first – 8 May – would be known as VE Day (short for Victory in Europe Day), and street parties were organized all over the country.

Sylvia Bell, Surbiton, aged 10

So there was this great adventure ahead of me: no war. And we didn't really know what was coming, we just knew that everyone was happy, very happy. And we read in the papers – by this time I think I was allowed to read the papers – and we read in the papers that war was over. Everyone was so very happy, so elated and so relieved, and this got over to the children and we were terribly happy the War was over. We didn't know what was coming because we couldn't remember what there was before. We just knew there was something great coming; things were going to be different.

Sylvia Limburg, evacuee in Wales, aged 10

I came home to London just for the VE Day celebrations. There were street parties in Fernhead Road where I lived and I was certainly there for those. They had a talent contest. I remember I was entered for the talent contest by my father and I belted [out] 'You Are My Sunshine' and I came second. A boy came first and I came second. And they also had a bonfire in the middle of the road.

Richard Faint, Lambeth, south London, aged 19

I remember all the flags and streamers across the street, banners up. Everywhere you seemed to go there were banners up or sheets hanging out windows: 'Welcome home, son.' They were everywhere. 'Welcome home, Dad.' Every street had organized parties and usually they were trestle tables and benches: lemonade and cakes, home-made cakes, fairy cakes and big currant cakes. It seemed everyone had salmon and shrimp paste sandwiches. And all the flags, flags everywhere, lots and lots of flags.

A VE celebration street party

Nothing to eat

Many Germans described 1945 as 'Year Zero', meaning that it was a time when their country had to begin all over again. Many of Germany's cities, including Berlin, had been completely devastated by bombing and heavy fighting. The damage was far worse than anything seen in Britain, and the country was in complete chaos. About a quarter of the entire population was homeless and few of Germany's main roads or railway lines were still intact. Vast columns of German prisoners of war trudged along rubble-strewn roads towards Allied prison camps. Millions of homeless refugees also trekked across the country, together with liberated Allied prisoners of war and foreign workers who had been held captive by the Nazis and were now trying to return home.

Edith Warthold, walked 200 km from Dresden to her home in Breslau with her mother and five schoolfriends

The railway lines were totally torn up and bent and there were no trains from there. So we started walking and it was a long way. Each night we had to find some place to stay. Sometimes we would stay in some farm, some kind family would take us in. Or sometimes we had to stay in ruins. And we had to be very quiet at night so nobody would find us. The Russians were there and we had to be very, very careful where we would go because people were for ever being attacked and shot, and all kinds of things happened.

> Soviet soldiers had fought a long and terribly bitter war since their country had been invaded, and they had seen with their own eyes how the Nazis had treated people in occupied Russia and Poland. They had also been fed a constant diet of anti-German propaganda from their own Communist Government, and when they finally reached Germany, many of them took their revenge on German civilians.

We had nothing to eat, nothing to drink. So we used to go on to fields and we dug out potatoes or whatever was still there. And water we found occasionally somewhere.

We were on the way for about three weeks, and we passed some dreadful sights. There were animals that had died, either because of starvation or injuries. The stench was unbearable. Sometimes there were humans who were lying there. So we just passed all that. We looked at it and we passed it. And we just went on and on and on.

Sometimes Russians would pass by lorry. Well, they didn't do us any harm but they were jeering and shouting and so on. One day we were sitting somewhere on the roadside and a few Russians were on the other side. One begged us to come over and my mother said, 'Don't go, don't go.' And then he showed us some bread, a big piece of Russian bread, and he said, 'Come, come.' So we went over and he gave us a piece of bread each and I thought it was very kind. Some Russians were very bad but he was one good person. But it didn't happen very often because there was not much to eat for anyone.

On our way, we found a small kind of hand-truck, a small wooden vehicle, four little wheels, and we thought it would carry our few belongings. (My mother had a bag and we still had our school satchels – of course there were no school books, we threw those away!) There was one girl, Eva, she was the smallest of all of us and she could hardly walk. So we found this little carriage and we put her on there and everybody was pushing and pulling. [And] we pulled it along all the way to Breslau.

Of course Breslau was totally destroyed. My mother said, 'Let's go to see…' – one of her friends. Their house was still standing and somebody let us in and said, 'Oh, you can just go in any of these flats. Just go and take a flat and you can stay here, it's up to you.' So we stayed there a few days. There was bedding and furniture because people just had to leave everything behind when they left Breslau to be evacuated. And you could find a coat and some shoes – but nothing to eat.

My mother had then to go every morning and had to work to clear ruins. There were mainly teams of about eight to ten women. The Polish army would take them along somewhere and say, 'Right you clear that ruin and you clear this street.' So all women were more or less employed by the authorities to clear the rubble – by hand – to make the streets accessible. And the women would get [paid] a very small amount.

Parts of eastern Germany, including Breslau, were occupied by Polish troops after the War and eventually incorporated into Poland. Most fit German men who had not been killed fighting were now in prisoner of war camps, so it was largely women who cleared the streets of German cities. They became known as *Trümmerfrauen* – 'Women of the Rubble.'

So we had to resort to going in ruins and taking things out. My mother said, 'You're old enough. You can do that. Go to the ruins and find whatever you think will be sellable on the black market.' So I went to different houses, and I found dolls, or maybe a shirt, or anything which was still in good condition. And I went regularly to the black market and we had to be very careful because it was illegal. But it was the only way of getting money and getting something to eat.

The conditions did not improve. We had something like Salvation Army soup kitchens. And you could go there and get a bowl of soup and a piece of bread. And my mother had to sell her wedding ring to get some money so we could buy some food.

Germans had to live among ruins for several years before their cities were reconstructed under the supervison of the occupying Allied powers. Acute food shortages also persisted and there was widespread hunger and disease, especially in Berlin.

From 1945 until 1948, many more refugees arrived as millions of German-speaking people from countries that had been occupied by Germany – including Poland, Hungary and Czechoslovakia – were forcibly expelled. In Czechoslovakia, some Germans were beaten up in the street and forced to wear painted swastikas on their coats – despite the fact that most had been living in the country since long before the War. Some were even shot, simply because they were German.

Eventually, in 1949, Germany was divided into two halves: West Germany (allied with Britain, France and the United States), and East Germany (allied with the Soviet Union).

After 1945

1945–7 The Soviet Union and the United States use their victories in the War to extend their influence. People in Soviet-occupied eastern Europe now find themselves living under another dictatorship.

1948 Worldwide horror at the Nazis' treatment of Jews helps bring about a Jewish State of Israel in Palestine. For the first time, Jews will have their own country with their own government and armed forces. But the Arabs of the Middle East oppose this, and in the ensuing war – which Israel wins – many Palestinian Arabs are forced to leave their homes and become refugees. The conflict continues today.

1948–1991 Mistrust and rivalry between the Soviet Union and the United States (allies during the war) leads to the 'Cold War'. This is a period of constant tension between the 'superpowers' resulting in an uneasy peace in Europe, and several wars elsewhere – including Korea, Vietnam and the Middle East.

1990s– With the collapse of the Soviet Union in 1991, the Cold War ends. However, wars continue to be fought around the globe and, as a result of conflicts rooted in the Second World War, they also break out in the part of Europe once known as Yugoslavia. Genocide (the attempt to murder a whole group of people with a particular racial, cultural or religious identity) also occurs, both in former Yugoslavia and in Rwanda (in Africa).

Afterword

All together, around 55 million people were killed during the Second World War, including some 20 million civilians. (Six million of those were Jews murdered by the Nazis.) It was the world's biggest military conflict and by far the most destructive.

Although the War ended in 1945, its effects continued to be felt long afterwards and still shape our world today. Similarly, for many of those children who survived the War, their personal experiences shaped the rest of their lives and profoundly affected their outlook on life. A few would rather forget, but most see it as vital to pass on their memories to future generations, in the hope that greater understanding will make such things less likely to happen again. It is mainly for that reason that the people in this book have agreed to speak to the Imperial War Museum about their experiences.

Unfortunately, millions of children all over the world have endured warfare – or the consequences of warfare – since 1945, and many are doing so today.

They have their own stories to tell.

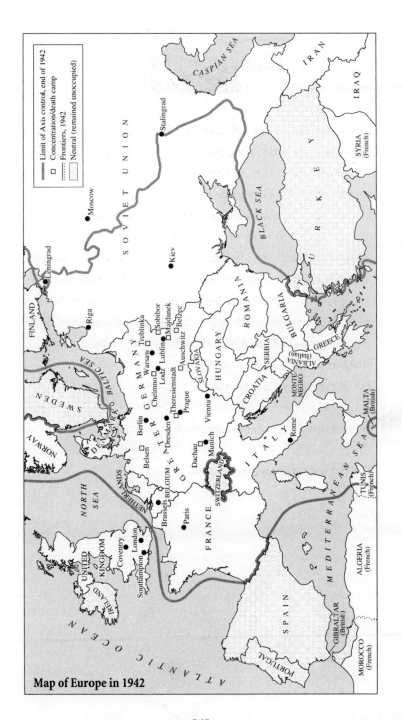

Map of Europe in 1942

Limit of Axis control, end of 1942
Concentration/death camp
Frontiers, 1942
Neutral (remained unoccupied)

ATLANTIC OCEAN

IRELAND
UNITED KINGDOM
Coventry
London
Southampton

NORTH SEA

NORWAY
SWEDEN
DENMARK
BALTIC SEA
FINLAND
Leningrad
Riga

SOVIET UNION
Moscow
Stalingrad
CASPIAN SEA
Kiev

NETHERLANDS
Brussels
BELGIUM
GREATER GERMANY
Belsen
Berlin
Dresden
Dachau
Munich
Theresienstadt
Prague
Chelmno
Lodz
Warsaw
Treblinka
Sobibor
Majdanek
Lublin
Belzec
Auschwitz
Vienna
SLOVAKIA
HUNGARY

Paris
FRANCE
SWITZERLAND
ITALY
Rome

ROMANIA
SERBIA
CROATIA
MONTE-NEGRO
BULGARIA
ALBANIA (Italian)
GREECE
BLACK SEA

TURKEY
IRAN
IRAQ
SYRIA (French)

PORTUGAL
SPAIN
GIBRALTAR (British)
MOROCCO (French)
ALGERIA (French)
TUNIS (French)
MEDITERRANEAN SEA
MALTA (British)

Suggested Reading

Fiction

Nina Bawden, *Carrie's War* (Puffin Modern Classics, 1993)

Judith Kerr, *Out Of The Hitler Time* (Including *When Hitler Stole Pink Rabbit* and *Bombs On Aunt Dainty*) (Harper Collins, 1994)

Michelle Magorian, *Goodnight Mister Tom* (Puffin Modern Classics, 1996)

Ian Serraillier, *The Silver Sword* (Puffin Modern Classics, 1993)

Robert Westall, *The Machine-Gunners* (Macmillan Children's Books, 2001)

Diaries/Memoirs

Anne Frank, *The Diary Of A Young Girl* (Puffin Modern Classics, 1998)

Laurel Holliday (editor), *Children's Wartime Diaries: Secret Writings From The Holocaust And World War II* (Washington Square Press, 1996)

Colin Perry, *Boy In The Blitz: The 1940 Diary Of Colin Perry* (Sutton Publishing, 2000)

Elie Wiesel, *Night* (Penguin, 1981)

General non-fiction

Matthew Hughes and Chris Mann, *Inside Hitler's Germany: Life Under The Third Reich* (Brown Reference Group, 2004)

Milton Meltzer, *Never To Forget: The Jews Of The Holocaust* (Harper Collins, 1976)

Karen Levine, *Hana's Suitcase* (Second Story Press, 2002)

Barbara Rogasky, *Smoke And Ashes: The Story Of The Holocaust* (Revised and expanded edition. Holiday House, Inc, 2002)

Barry Turner, *One Small Suitcase: The True Story Of How 10,000 Children Escaped The Nazi Holocaust* (Puffin Books, 2003)

Robert Westall, *Children Of The Blitz: Memories Of Wartime Childhood* (Revised edition: Macmillan Children's Books, 1995)

All interviews have been edited. The Imperial War Museum catalogue numbers of the original interviews are given here, along with interviewees' married or adopted names. Interviews marked [OF] were conducted by October Films. Interviews conducted by the Imperial War Museum are marked [IWM].

Anonymous girl, Stuttgart (10554) [IWM] 16, 26, 31, 219, 236–8, 250–1

Jack Aizenberg (15536) [IWM] 256

Waltraudt Asser (Waltraudt Williams 10110) [IWM] 20, 34, 44, 218–19, 221, 253–5

Gerda Ballin (Gerda Dales 4599) [IWM] 33

Hana Bandler (16684) [IWM] 50

Lawrence Beaumont (14149) [IWM] 176

Derek Bech (23832) [IWM] 149–53

Sonia Bech (Sonia Williams 23173) [IWM] 152

Sylvia Bell (Sylvia Taylor 5382) [IWM] 88–9, 163, 179, 232, 258

Ryvka Berkowicz (Ryvka Salt 15622) [IWM] 190, 246–7

Oliver Bernard (11481) [IWM] 161–3, 180

Tauba Biber (19792) [OF] 103, 105–6, 202, 210, 214

Renee Bore (Renee Ponsford 18460) [IWM] 164, 168–9, 179

Franz Brichta (Frank Bright 16841) [IWM] 201–2, 204

Margaret Butler (Margaret Woodhead 5380) [IWM] 77, 128, 223–4, 227–8, 230

Edward Butt (5225) [IWM] 89, 178, 232, 235

Charles Carrington (21052) [IWM] 130–1

Joan Chantrelle (Joan Reed 5390) [IWM] 70, 73, 76, 78, 80, 85, 92–4

Arthur Dales (14595) [IWM] 172, 175, 177

Janina Dawidowicz (Janina David 9538) [IWM] 103, 108–10, 113–15, 117, 189, 194

Margarit Dierksen (Margarit Young 22914) [IWM] 12–13, 15, 19–20, 45, 60, 218, 239–40, 245–6, 251, 255

Shmuel Dresner (9136) [IWM] 114, 116

Herbert Eisenthal (Herbert Elliott 16484) [IWM] 39–40

Bertha Engelhard (Bertha Leverton 17310) [IWM] 50

Inge Engelhard (Ingeborg Sadan 17290) [IWM] 53–4, 56–7, 133, 170–1

Richard Faint (14145) [IWM] 167–9, 258–9

Kitty Felix (Kitty Hart-Moxon 19784) [OF] 106–9, 112–13, 118–20, 186, 200, 203–4, 206–9, 211–13

Wiebke Fick (Wiebke Stammers 9089) [IWM] 12, 14, 16–17, 20–2, 25

Peter Frank (16690) [IWM] 185–6

Henry Fulda (12262) [IWM] 134

May George (May Moore 6353) [IWM]

Szmulek Gontarz (10348) [IWM] 75

Alicia Gornowski (9241) [IWM] 192–3

Pauline de Guerrin (Pauline Harris 17364) [IWM] 142

Roman Halter (19786) [OF] 104–5, 109, 188, 190–1, 199, 211–13

Dennis Hayden (5266) [IWM] 69, 88, 148, 229

Walter Hayman (4482) [IWM] 132

Ruth Heilbron (Ruth Foster 19782) [OF] 29–30, 184–5

Eric Hill (12673) [IWM] 131, 172

Klara Hochhauser (Clare Parker 14864) [IWM] 256

Hildegard Hornblower (8264) [IWM] 22–3

Barbara Isralowitz (Barbara Eaton 4380) [IWM] 28, 45, 48–9, 58, 134

Edyta Klein (Edyta Klein-Smith 19785) [OF] 103, 107, 109, 111–12, 117, 120, 188–9, 191–2

Magdalena Kusserow (Magdalena Kusserow Reuter 19793) [OF] 30–1

Sylvia Limburg (Sylvia Townson 5417) [IWM] 146, 166, 235, 258

Rena Litwak (Rena Zabielak 17369) [IWM] 107

Elisabeth Lukas (Elisabeth Lucas-Harrison 8304) [IWM] 15–16, 27–8, 34, 96–8

Alan Maynard (5260) [IWM] 129

Desmond McGarry (10713) [IWM] 136–8

Ronald McGill (6221) [IWM] 71, 73, 77, 88, 160–2, 169, 172–3, 229, 233–6

Stella Metcalfe (Stella Perkins 10105) [IWM] 137–8

Henry Metelmann (8171) [IWM] 14, 18–19, 25, 31–2, 39–40, 60

Derek Milton (11451) [IWM] 128, 147–8, 164–6, 180, 231

Berek Obuchowski (9203) [IWM] 193, 255

Dorothy Oppenheimer (Dorothy Fleming 16600) [IWM] 39, 46, 50–2, 133–4

Margie Oppenheimer (17759) [IWM] 42

Susan Oppenheimer (Susan Sinclair 17177) [IWM] 27, 42, 46–8, 57–8

Albin Ossowski (19795) [OF] 118

Armand Otto Jakubovic (16695) [IWM] 210

Sylvia Parkes (Sylvia Hadley 5213) [IWM] 84, 86–7, 90, 127, 170–1

Josef Perl (17883) [IWM] 187, 213

Helen Pieper (Helena Leach 10306) [IWM] 14

Stan Poole (22198) [IWM] 131, 176, 223

Walter Rechnitzer (Walter Richards 17355) [IWM] 43, 50

Colin Ryder Richardson (20805) [IWM] 150–1, 153–6

Joanna Rogers (Joanna Lawrence 6013) [IWM] 65, 78, 125, 143–8, 163–4, 222, 224–6, 228–31, 233

Issy Rondell (10303) [IWM] 117–18

Gerti Seewald (16505) [IWM] 58

Muriel Shean (Muriel Tucker 5261) [IWM] 67, 69

Maria Siegel (Maria Green 16784) [IWM] 41, 46, 52–4, 56–7, 172

John Silbermann (18672) [IWM] 58

Gisela Spanglet (Gisela Eisner 14763) [IWM] 24, 55

Heinz Spanglet (Stephen Dale 14582) [IWM] 33

Kenneth Sparks (22230) [IWM] 150, 155

Barbara Stimler (19787) [OF] 103, 105, 107, 199–201, 203–4, 210, 214

Graham Swain (22352) [IWM] 175

Hannah Voss (Hannah Hyde 10380) [IWM] 252, 257

Edith Warthold (Edith St Romaine 15751) [IWM] 245, 248–50, 260–2

Gwendoline Watts (Gwendoline Stewart 5334) [IWM] 71, 73, 77, 80, 91, 94–5, 174, 177, 179

Irene Weller (Irene Mead 5343) [IWM] 64, 67–71, 74–6, 78–79, 85, 87, 95

Jutta Zelle (Jutta Buder 22580) [IWM] 220, 237–8, 244, 251

air raids 62, 66, 84, 145–8, 157–80, 218–22, 237–8, 241, 247–50, 252

Anderson shelters 145, 164, 179

anti-Semitism 22, 24, 26, 59, 99, 111

ARP (Air Raid Precautions) wardens 66, 174–8

Aryans 18, 20, 22, 25, 30

Atlantic Ocean 139, 149–50, 152, 215, 224

Auschwitz 182, 186, 195, 197–214, 241

Australia 49, 62, 122, 135

Austria 35, 38–40, 64

Axis powers 121

barrage balloons 127

Belgium 48–9, 55, 81, 95–4, 97–8, 100, 182, 196, 216

blackouts 66, 80, 92–3

Blitz 157–8, 165–7, 169, 180, 237

blitzkrieg (lightning war) 102, 157

bomb shelters 61–2, 125, 145, 161–4, 166–7, 174, 177–9, 219–20, 238

Britain 9, 32, 35–6, 41, 45, 47
    and Auschwitz 213
    Battle of 139–40, 142–9, 155, 157–8, 173
    bombing of 215–16
    evacuation 64, 81–2, 121–2, 124, 126, 131, 135
    Phoney War 98
    pre-war 49–50, 55, 57–60, 62
    victory 258–9

call-up 223

Canada 49, 122, 129, 135, 139–40, 149–50, in Auschwitz 208

carpet bombing 221

Chamberlain, Neville 35, 41, 45, 62, 79, 81, 121

Channel Islands 122, 136, 138

Christians 22, 29, 31, 99

Churchill, Winston 81, 121, 128–9, 136, 139–40, 157, 166, 231, 247

City of Benares (evacuation ship) 140, 149–56

Communist Party 32, 181, 260

concentration camps 31–2, 40, 43, 47, 51, 104, 182, 185, 195–6, 198, 241, 246, 255, 257

Coventry 158, 171

curfew 185

cyanide gas 202

Czechoslovakia 35–6, 40–1, 59–60, 64, 140

D-Day 216, 229–30, 235–6

death camps 182, 187, 190, 196

Denmark 81, 100

deportation 184, 186–7, 189, 194

Der Stürmer (Nazi newspaper) 23–4, 30

Dig for Victory 125, 224

Dresden 180, 241, 247–50

Dunkirk 81–2, 97–8, 121, 124, 127–9

Eisenhower, General 242

England 46, 49, 56, 98, 136, 139–40, 157

evacuation 61–81, 84–95, 122, 124, 126–7, 129, 140, 149–50, 155, 221–2

Final Solution 181–2, 195–6, 213

First World War 9–10, 60, 64, 102, 115

flying bombs 216, 236

France 9–10, 35–6, 41, 49, 55, 59–60, 62, 81, 95–8, 100, 104, 109, 121, 125, 136, 182, 196, 216, 234

Frank, Anne 186

gas chambers 185, 189, 195–6, 198, 202, 204–5, 207, 211, 213–14, 241

gas masks 61, 64, 66, 84–5, 240
Germany 9–10, 14, 18–22, 27, 31–2
  Axis powers 121–2
  bombing of 216, 218
  Channel Islands 138
  death camps 195, 208, 213
  Final Solution 181, 184, 195
  invasion of Poland 67, 79
  Phoney War 81, 98–9
  post D-Day 236–7, 239–42, 244–5
  pre-war 36, 38–42, 45–6, 48–9, 51, 55–62
  propaganda 133
  surrender of 250, 252, 255, 257–60
Gestapo (Hitler's secret police) 30, 32–3,
  185–6, 190
ghettos 99–120, 181–94, 196, 198, 210
Girl Guides 143–4
GIs (US soldiers) 227
Goebbels, Josef (Nazi Minister of
  Propaganda) 22, 218
Greater Germany 36, 38, 42, 184, 186
guided missiles 231
Gypsies 30–1, 196, 198

Himmler, Heinrich (leader of SS) 104, 194
Hiroshima 242
Hitler, Adolf 7, 9–10, 12–23, 27–30, 32–3,
  35–6, 38–42, 47, 57, 59–62, 64, 81–2,
  85, 95, 98–9, 104, 106, 121, 124, 129,
  133, 136, 139, 157–8, 165–6, 181, 184,
  196, 215–16, 218–19, 221, 227, 231–2,
  235, 241–2, 244, 250, 252, 254–5
Hitler Youth 18–22, 24–5, 32, 219, 221,
  237, 254
Holland 53, 55, 81, 95–6, 98, 100, 104,
  131, 182, 196
Home Guard (see also *Volkssturm*) 121,
  129–31, 177

incendiary bombs 162, 171, 176–9, 249
internment 121, 133–6, 138
Isle of Man 133–4
Israel 107
Italy 35, 46, 121, 196, 216

Japan 180–1, 242
Jehovah's Witnesses 30–1
Jewish Question 106, 181–2
Jews 9–10, 15, 18, 22–3, 25–32, 34–6,
  42–9, 56–7, 59, 96, 98–120, 181–96, 198

kapos 210–12
Kindertransport 36, 49, 51, 55, 58
Korczak, Janusz (Polish educator and
  writer) 191
Kristallnacht 36, 43, 45–6

labour camps 99, 138, 182, 189, 205, 246
Little Blitz 216, 230
Local Defence Volunteers 121, 129
Lodz ghetto 100, 109, 112–13, 188, 190, 193
London Underground 167–9
Lublin ghetto 109, 112
Luftwaffe (German air force) 139–40,
  145, 157–8, 161, 164, 169, 216, 230
Luxembourg 81, 100

Make Do and Mend 225
master race 18, 22
Mein Kampf 9, 18
messenger boys 174–7
Ministry of Food 225
Munich Agreement 35–6, 41, 59, 61

Nagasaki 242
Nazi (National Socialist) Party 9
  death camps 196, 198, 202, 207, 209–10

early wartime 98, 100, 104–5, 107, 109, 111–12, 116, 120
ghettos 181–2, 184–6, 189, 191, 193
pre-war 10, 12, 20–1, 24–6, 29–33, 35–6, 39, 42, 44–6, 51–3, 59, 61
salute 14, 16–17, 20–1, 27–8
surrender 246, 254–5, 257, 260
Normandy landings 230
Norway 13, 81, 100
Nuremberg rallies 21, 242

Olympic Games 20
Operation Sea Lion 139

Palestine 46–7, 49, 107
Panzerfaust (German anti-tank rocket launcher) 254
Pathé (newsreels) 125
Pearl Harbor 181
Phoney War 81, 98
Poland 18, 36, 60, 62, 67, 79, 81, 99–100, 102, 104, 106, 109–10, 140, 181–2, 185–6, 195–6, 198, 241, 260
propaganda 22–3, 25–6, 40, 218, 252, 260

rabbis 105
RAF (Royal Air Force) 139–40, 143–4, 157, 215, 221, 237
rationing 85–6, 149, 218, 226, 240, 251
Red Cross 250
resettlement 185, 187, 189, 191, 193
Romania 100, 182
Royal Navy 121, 128, 149, 153
Rumkowski, Chaim (leader of Lodz Ghetto) 193
Russia 18, 32, 104, 181

St Paul's Cathedral 158, 173

selections 189–93, 200, 205, 211–13
Slavs 18, 104
Soviet Union 18, 99, 157, 181–2, 184–5, 215, 241, 244, 260
Spitfire Fund 143
Squander Bug 225
SS (elite Nazi soldiers) 104, 113, 184–5, 187, 189–91, 194, 198, 200, 205, 208, 210–12, 214, 244, 253
Stalin, Josef 99
Stalingrad, Battle of 215, 218
Star of David 100, 107, 182, 186
Storm Troopers 12, 21, 25–6, 32, 42–3
street parties 258–9
Strength Through Joy 13, 246
surrender 242, 250, 254–5, 258
swastika 12
Switzerland 49

tattoos 203–4, 213
telegrams 236
tip-and-run raids 221

U-boats 139–40, 149–50, 215, 224
United States 9–10, 34–5, 45–6, 49, 55, 122, 129, 181, 213–15, 235, 242, 252
United States Air Force 229

V1 rockets 216, 231–4
V2 rockets 216, 234–5
VE (Victory in Europe) Day 242, 258
Volkssturm (German Home Guard) 254

war crimes 242
Warsaw ghetto 100, 109–11, 114–15, 117–19, 188–9, 191, 193–4
Wehrmacht (German army) 104

Picture credits

P13 HU6339; P15 HU6299; P17 NYP68053; P19 HU6296; P21 HU6301; P24 HU6312;
P26 MH13348; P29 GER305; P38 NYP68062; P40 NYP68064; P43 HU82950;
P44 FRA204717; P59 MH13116; P65 HU36124; P66 D3162; P68 S&G30491;
P70 HU36238; P72 AP7455B; P74 HU63760; P76 D3106; P86 HU63757;
P89 HU36218; P90 HU36236; P92 MH6712; P97 F4499; P102 HU6343;
P108 IA37590; P114 HU60614; P116 HU60701; P124 C1741; P126 HU82264;
P128 H9148; P130 HU82341; P132 IWM PST0142; P144 HU36152; P147 HU62262;
P154 HU54058; P161 HU1129; P162 D24235; P165 D3171; P167 PL14560;
P168 PL11627; P170 PL4511A; P173 HU36220; P175 D2629; P178 HU36129;
P188 IA37578; P205 HU90295; P220 HU 55455; P222 D8573; P222 D20152;
P225 IWM PST6080; P228 NYT27247; P232 HU36294; P234 HU36227;
P239 MH27656; P245 HU55499; P253 HU55487; P254 NYP62569; P256 BU3810
All Imperial War Museum

P247 HU3321 Imperial War Museum/Goetz Bergander; P259 HU49482 Imperial
War Museum/Fox Photos; P23 Mary Evans/Weimar Archive; P52 Ingeborg Sadan/
Bertha Leverton; P51 The Wiener Library; P55 The Wiener Library; P111 akg-
images, London; P119 akg-images, London; P156 Illustrated London News; P192
akg-images, London; P198 akg-images, London, P201 Yad Vashem Archive; P203
Yad Vashem Archive; P205 Yad Vashem Archive; P265 András Bereznay

Other sources used in this book

Beevor, Antony, *Berlin: The Downfall 1945* (London: Penguin, 2002); Burleigh,
Michael, *The Third Reich: A New History* (London: Macmillan, 2000); Calder, Angus,
The People's War: Britain 1939–1945 (London: Jonathan Cape, 1969); Dawidowicz,
Lucy, *The War Against The Jews, 1933–1945* (London: Weidenfeld & Nicolson, 1975);
Gilbert, Martin, *Never Again: A History Of The Holocaust* (London: Harper Collins,
2000); Parsons, Martin, and Penny Starns, *The Evacuation: The True Story* (DSM,
1999); Turner, Barry, *...And The Policeman Smiled: 10,000 Children Escape From
Nazi Europe* (London: Bloomsbury, 1990); Ziegler, Philip, *London At War 1939–1945*
(London: Random House, 1997)